D0955664

PATRIOTISM IN AMERICA

Patriotism is worn in the heart and not on the sleeve.

— *Tom Wicker, columnist, the New York Times*

PATRIOTISM IN AMERICA

BY

GERALD LEINWAND

DEMOCRACY IN ACTION

FRANKLIN WATTS

A Division of Grolier Publishing

New York • London • Hong Kong • Sydney

Danbury, Connecticut

Interior Design by Claire Fontaine

Photographs ©: AP/Wide World Photos: 22, 47, 94, 144; Archive Photos: Culver Pictures: 3; 32 (Lambert), 37, 57, 68, 72, 79, 89, 138; Corbis-Bettmann: 62, 120; North Wind Picture Archives: 103, 114; UPI/Corbis-Bettmann: 13, 99, 106, 127.

Library of Congress Cataloging-in-Publication Data

Leinwand, Gerald
Patriotism in America / by Gerald Leinwand.
p. cm. — (Democracy in action)
Includes bibliographical references and index.
Summary: Examines the elements of the unifying phenomenon of patriotism in the United States.
ISBN 0-531-11310-8
1. Patriotism—United States. [1. Patriotism.]
I. Title. II. Series: Democracy in action (Franklin Watts, Inc.)
JK1759.L54 1997
320.5'4'0973—dc20 96-34942
CIP
AC

Printed in the United States of America

1 2 3 4 5 6 7 8 9 10 R 06 05 04 03 02 01 00 99 98 97

Table of Contents

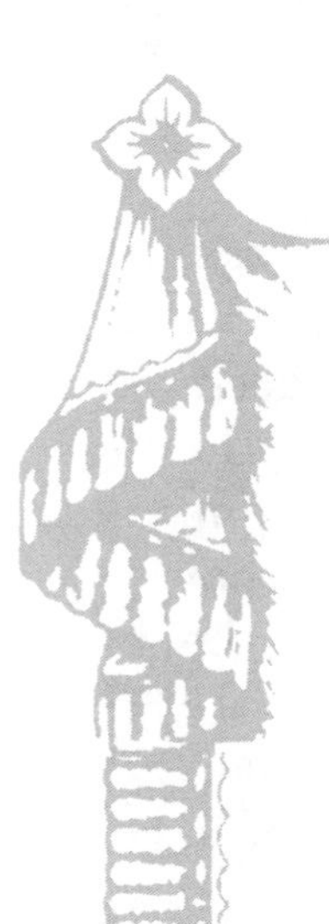

PROLOGUE

THE AMERICAN MIRACLE

I pledge allegiance to the flag of the United States of America and to the republic for which it stands, one nation under God, indivisible, with liberty and justice for all.

The miracle we take for granted is that while other nations were formed on the basis of race, ethnicity, national origins, or a common religion, language, or history, America was formed on the basis of a set of overarching ideas. While other nations have had the benefit of shared victories and defeats, shared heroes and heroines, common memories, and familiar songs, stories, and legends, America had to manufacture its own. Great ideas as expressed in such historic documents as the Declaration of Independence and the Constitution or in speeches by George Washington, Abraham Lincoln, or the Reverend Martin Luther King Jr. have kept a diverse people united and the nation indivisible. When we salute the flag, we are not merely expressing devotion to our country, important as that is; we are also recognizing the republican ideas of liberty and justice for which it stands.

The miracle of America is that while in modern Europe, Africa, and Latin America patriotism has served to fragment nations—that is, to divide them into rival camps with seemingly insurmountable ethnic grudges and religious hatreds—in the United States patriotism has united a land of continental proportions and a people from every section of the globe.

This did not happen all at once, however. At different times in our history, fragmentation seemed inevitable as various parts of the country tested the ties that bound the fledgling nation together. In 1806 Aaron Burr, while still vice president of the United States, conspired to create a nation west of the Mississippi with himself as president or king. President Thomas Jefferson accused Burr of treason, but Burr was acquitted of that charge. Nevertheless, his rather bizarre adventure illustrated that a united nation was by no means a sure thing. Nor would it be for some time. In 1814, New England, fearing that the United States would lose the War of 1812, attempted to make its own peace with England.

In 1861 the Confederacy sought secession so that it could preserve slavery. This was the major challenge to the young nation. The North's victory assured the end of slavery and the survival of the

American union. But the cost of such a victory was substantial.

In 1863, while the Civil War was still raging and victory for the Union cause remained elusive, Edward Everett Hale wrote "The Man without a Country." The main character of the short story is Lieutenant Philip Nolan, who has been court-martialed for cooperating with Aaron Burr, the would-be traitor to the United States.

In a moment of uncontrollable anger, Nolan curses the United States and expresses the wish never to hear its name again. His punishment is to have his wish granted. He is banished and ordered to spend the rest of his life on a naval vessel where all who have contact with him are instructed never to mention the United States. As he ages, the torment grows, and on his deathbed he realizes what his country really meant to him. To be without a country "is as hideous a form of leprosy as the imagination can contrive."[1] So it was in 1863; so it is today.

The end of the Civil War in 1865 clinched the idea that this was an indivisible nation of indissoluble states. For more than two hundred years—a period that has included a revolution, a civil war, two world wars, a great depression, and a generous immigration policy that has attracted men and women from every corner of the world—the United States has lived up to its motto, *E Pluribus Unum* (one from many). But as we approach the 21st century will America continue to be indivisible? At home, separatist currents are beginning to erode the concept of an indivisible nation, and there are some who question whether an indivisible nation is worth saving. Abroad, the breakup of the old Soviet Union and the former Yugoslavia are examples of the formidable currents that can destroy nations, currents from which America may not be immune.

Because, in the poet Robert Penn Warren's words, "to be an American is not . . . a matter of blood; it is a matter of an idea,"[2] in this volume we will examine some of the elements of American patriotism that make an indivisible nation possible. These will include the great ideas by which Americans live, as well as the symbols, the myths, the monuments, and the holidays by which we symbolically express national pride, commemorate important events in America's history, and inspire a new generation of Americans.

ONE

WHAT IS PATRIOTISM?

This monument marks the first burying ground in Plymouth of the passengers of the Mayflower. Here, under cover of darkness, the fast dwindling company lay their dead, leveling the earth above them lest the Indians should learn how many were the graves. History records no nobler venture for faith and freedom than of this Pilgrim band. . . . May their example inspire thee to do thy part in perpetuating and spreading the lofty ideals of our republic throughout the world.

—Inscription on Plymouth Rock Monument, Plymouth, Massachusetts

At its best, patriotism is one of the noblest of human sentiments. At its worst, as the 18th-century English writer Samuel Johnson reminds us, it is "the last refuge of the scoundrel." Between these two extremes lies a vast range of patriotic emotion. Although some scoundrels may have wrapped themselves in the cloak of patriotism, patriotism remains the cement that binds any society together. Without patriotism a society becomes unstuck. Without patriotism religious, ethnic, regional, and self-interest groups go their separate ways, making it difficult, if not altogether impossible, for a people to get on with their tasks. Without patriotism, including its symbols and its many forms of expression, society stumbles and disintegrates.

Patriotism Defined

Patriotism is love of one's country. It is love of the land where one is born or the land to which one gives allegiance. According to historian Dixon Wecter, "Patriotism springs traditionally from love of place; it is a filial relation toward mother country or fatherland. The earth upon which our feet are planted, from which we draw our livelihood, becomes an over-soul, the greatest hero of our national loyalties."[1] While patriotism begins with love of land, it also encompasses love of familiar customs, unique traditions, and special missions of a people. John Adams said that the American Revolution took place in the hearts and minds of the American people long before a shot was fired. He meant that long before the outbreak of the War for Independence, the colonists began to think of themselves as living in a separate land, having their own distinct traditions, and having a world mission different from that of England, the country from which most of the colonists had come.

Patriotism leads to sacrifice. At one extreme, patriotism asks, "Are you willing to die for our country?" But it would be a grave mistake to conclude that patriotism requires only a willingness to lay down one's life for one's country. Instead, patriotism urges

Flags flutter over a ticker-tape parade for Persian Gulf veterans held on June 10, 1996, in New York City.

the individual to put national interest ahead of self-interest, ahead of personal or material gain. It requires that short-term gratification be deferred so that the long-term interests of the nation and of future generations may ultimately be achieved.

Patriotism, nationalism, loyalty, and Americanism are interrelated. Whereas patriotism is rooted in love of the land, nationalism focuses on the desire to set up a government to rule that land in accordance with its special geographic, economic, social, and political characteristics. Nationalism refers to the state, its form of government, its territorial extent, the conduct of its domestic and foreign affairs. When Dr. Johnson said that "patriotism is the last refuge of a scoundrel" he really meant nationalism, a term that did not become meaningful until many years after his death. Patriotism is never a substitute for a religious faith, but nationalism often is, as in the case of Nazi Germany or fascist Italy where the dictators sought to encourage worship of the state and themselves. Historian John Lukacs has observed, "[P]atriotism is essentially defensive, while nationalism is aggressive, and . . . the former is deeper rooted than the latter."[2] Patriotism is that element in nationalism that evokes a willingness of the people to be supportive of the nation.

Patriots make sacrifices to bring the nation into existence. They protect it from the external enemies and internal threats that may undermine or destroy it. Francis Scott Key, who wrote "The Star-Spangled Banner," caught this admixture of patriotism and nationalism in America in the third stanza of our national anthem: "Blessed with victory and peace, may the heaven rescued land; praise the power that has made and preserved us a nation." Or as Daniel Webster, a prominent senator, declared, "Let it be borne on the flag under which we rally in every exigency that we have one country, one constitution, one destiny."

Loyalty to the nation is patriotism. However, in America loyalty may be shared. One is loyal to family, friends, colleagues. One may be loyal to school, team, club, or professional association. And one may be loyal to one's beliefs, ideals, or religious affiliation. Just as scoundrels have sometimes wrapped themselves in the cloak of patriotism, so thieves have worn the mantle of loyalty. Street gangs, for example, often take elaborate measures to assure that their members will be steadfast or loyal.

Patriots have made a primary commitment of loyalty to the nation. He or she is willing to make sacrifices so that the nation might be saved from harm. In *A Preface to Morals*, Walter Lippmann, the distinguished and influential Pulitzer Prize–winning journalist, wrote:

> *[I]n the legends of heroes, of sages, of explorers, inventors and discoverers, of pioneers and patriots, there is almost invariably this same underlying theme of sacrifice and unworldliness. They are poor. They live dangerously. By ordinary standards they are extremely uncomfortable. They give up ease, property, pleasure, pride, place, and power to attain things which are transcendent and rare. They live for ends which seem to yield no profit and they are ready to die, if need be, for that which the dead can no longer enjoy.*[3]

At one extreme, loyalty may reach fanatic proportions as it did in Nazi Germany, where loyalty to the fatherland came before loyalty to the family, to one's religion, or to the truth. In the United States undivided loyalty was, at one time, regarded as the national ideal. Presidents Theodore Roosevelt and Woodrow

Case Study:
Saluting the Flag

During the late 1930s and early 1940s, a religious group known as the Jehovah's Witnesses challenged the authority of the states to require their children to salute the flag or to recite the Pledge of Allegiance during school assemblies. It was their belief that in so doing they were violating the Bible's second commandment, which forbids the worship of graven images.

In the case of *Minersville School District v. Gobitis* (1941), the U.S. Supreme Court ruled against the Jehovah's Witnesses, holding that a state had a right to require the salute and the recitation of the Pledge of Allegiance. As the threat of war mounted, the Witnesses were subject to verbal and physical abuse when they persisted in protesting the decision. But many Americans felt that in the *Gobitis* case the Court had gone much too far. Even as patriotic an organization as the American Legion sponsored a bill, eventually enacted by Congress in 1942, that provided: "civilians will show full respect to the flag when the pledge is given by merely standing at attention, men removing the headdress." The Jehovah's Witnesses had always expressed a willingness to comply to this extent.

In 1943, when World War II was at its peak, patriotism was encouraged as a means of building support for the war effort. In that year, although patriotism was running at fevered pitch, the Supreme Court in a 6–3 decision reversed itself, ruling that a West Virginia law requiring flag salute was an unconstitutional interference with religious freedom. Those whose religion required that they forego the pledge to the flag were free to abstain. In *West Virginia Board of Education v. Barnette*, Justice Robert H. Jackson wrote for the Court, "If there is any fixed star in our constitutional constellation, it is that no official, high or petty, can prescribe what shall be orthodox in politics, nationalism, religion, or other matters of opinion or force citizens to confess by word or act their faith therein." He went on to say, "The case is made difficult not because the principles of its decision are obscure but because the flag involved is our own. Nevertheless, we apply the limitations of the Constitution without fear. . . . To believe that patriotism will not flourish if patriotic ceremonies are voluntary is to make an unflattering estimate of the appeal of our institutions to free minds."

Wilson both scorned what they called the hyphenated Americans, that is, those immigrants who retained the traditions and the language of the countries from which they came instead of modeling their lives totally on idealized images of the Americans of 1776.

This pressure to conform has been called the "melting pot" theme of American history. This idea held that immigrants who came to these shores would quickly become something different from what they had been; they would become "American." This concept has been replaced by the idea of cultural pluralism, which expects a primary loyalty to America but does not require that one's origins, culture, roots, or traditions be ignored or belittled.

Characteristics of American Patriotism

The decision in the *Barnette* case reminds us that patriotism in America has a number of important characteristics. In the first instance, patriotism cannot be coerced. Neither the state nor the national government can require the participation of civilians in any public display of patriotic fervor.

American patriotism is acquired, not inherited. It is by no means confined to those whose families have lived in America for many generations. Indeed, some of the most patriotic men and women are those who have been here but a short time.

Organized expressions of American patriotism are mainly supported through private sources of funding. Most national patriotic monuments were paid through the private solicitation of funds.

Throughout most of America's history, patriotism grew without the nurturing from the military establishment. The military in America has always been relatively small and remains strictly subordinate to civilian authority. No officer class and no inherited titles of nobility, which in other countries take the cultivation of patriotism as their focus, have existed in America. Although patriotism in America has been erratic, it has been also, for the most part, peaceful in character and in expression.

Columnist Hendrick Hertzberg wrote in the *Nation* that patriotism in America "is not based on a mystique of blood and soil. It's not based on a commonality of race, religion, or even . . . 'national origin.' It is based quite explicitly on civil and political values: liberty of expression, democratic political institutions, civic equality and a secular state."[4]

Loyalty to the nation is essential to its survival and to the happiness of its people, yet the paradox of loyalty suggests that fanatical loyalty to a particular regime or to a set of rigidly held beliefs is inconsistent with America as a nation of free women and men. A citizen in a democracy, as noted by author Morton Grodzins, "has many other loyalties on which the strength of national loyalty depends."[5]

To Thomas Jefferson, Americanism meant those unique characteristics of the republican form of government that the Declaration of Independence inspired and the U.S. Constitution established. What was unique about America in 1789, the year George

Washington was first inaugurated as president, was that in a world of divine-right monarchs, the United States had set up a government with an elected president and elected representatives, all of whom were devoted, as the preamble of the Constitution clearly indicated, "to secure the blessings of Liberty to ourselves and our Posterity." Americanism that meant life, liberty, and the pursuit of happiness would be achieved not only through a republican form of government but also through separation of church and state, a market economy, and a tax-supported school system.

At times, Americanism as a term has strayed far from the meaning Jefferson gave it. It has been used by some to suggest expectations of blind obedience and rigid conformity to a single set of values believed to be "American." The term "un-American" has been sometimes applied to those who have different ideas as to what it means to be patriotic. So that we may better understand the nature of Americanism and what it means to be patriotic, let's examine the growth of American patriotism.

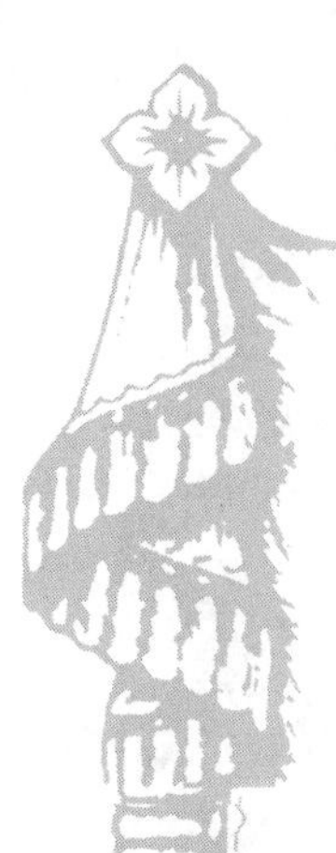

Two

How Did American Patriotism Grow?

It has often given me pleasure to observe that independent America was not composed of detached and distant territories. . . . Providence has in a particular manner blessed it with a variety of soils and productions and watered it with innumerable streams for the delight and accommodation of its inhabitants. A succession of navigable waterways forms a kind of chain around its borders, as if to bind it together; while the most noble rivers in the world, running at convenient distances, present them with highways for easy communication of friendly aids and the mutual transportation and exchange of their various commodities.[1]

—John Jay

The Declaration of Independence marked a sharp but logical expression of distinctively American patriotism. The steps that led colonists from thinking of themselves as subjects of England to thinking of themselves as citizens of America were relatively swift. "Thirteen clocks," John Adams said, "were made to strike together—a perfection of mechanism which no artist had ever before effected."[2] The miracle, for it seemed nothing less, was achieved without a previous national experience and after a colonial experience of little more than 150 years. Even the boundaries of the new land had not yet been entirely identified. Common customs and traditions were few, and these not fully formed. Nevertheless, religion and education—as well as the economy and geography of the new nation — contributed to the growth of American patriotism.

American Religion and American Patriotism

Patriotism is defined as love of the land, but its roots may be said to be based upon the love of God. Having crossed a treacherous ocean and having endured, in the words of William Bradford of Plymouth Colony, in a "harsh and desolate wilderness," there was a feeling that God had chosen the Puritans for some special purpose. Here was a "New World," a land of "milk and honey," which God had provided for his "chosen people," much as he had provided for the children of Israel, the "chosen people" of biblical days.

God, it was felt, had brought the Puritans to these distant shores and had imbued those who survived that first cruel winter with a divine mission to achieve something better here in America. According to Governor John Winthrop, the colonists of Massachusetts Bay Colony were "to build a city upon a hill" to reflect the greater glory of God and to free the New World from the corruption and tyranny of the old.

The idea that Americans are a chosen people has often been a theme repeated throughout U.S. history. In 1861, Lincoln referred to "this almost chosen people." A little more than a century later, President

This painting depicts the landing of the Pilgrims at Plymouth Rock in 1620.

Ronald Reagan declared, when addressing the nation on the eve of Thanksgiving in 1982, "I've always believed that this land was set aside in an uncommon way, that a divine plan placed this great continent between the oceans to be found by people from every corner of the earth who had a special love of faith, freedom and peace."

Destined by God, so they believed, to be a great and unique people, the colonists found in the Bible and their houses of worship the spiritual roots of American patriotism. During the process of making one nation out of thirteen colonies, religious institutions, despite their differing doctrines, sought to establish the ideal of religious freedom in a politically free nation. Aware of threats to religious liberty in the lands from which they or their ancestors had come, most clergy zealously supported the guarantee of religious liberty.

Throughout the formative years of the nation (1774–89), according to historian Edward F. Humphrey, "The pulpit was the most powerful force in America for the control of public opinion."[3] Preachers were central in molding public thought in every hamlet, village, and town. The church was a house of meeting as much as it was a house of worship. It was the light from a church steeple that told Paul Revere whether the British were coming, thus symbolically reinforcing the role of the church in the spirit of revolution. If, as John Adams said, the revolution began before the war because it was in the minds and hearts of the people, it was in their minds in a large measure because the nation's houses of worship had put it there. The preacher was the most powerful local politician of the day. It is difficult to see how the revolution's leaders could have won the support of church-going Americans without the significant support of religious leaders. Because most leaders saw the revolution as an opportunity to preserve religious independence, it was both wise and expedient for them to put their weight behind the new nation. By proclaiming the new nation's divine role, religious leaders helped develop loyalty to it.

At the Constitutional Convention itself, any discussion of religion was taboo. When Benjamin Franklin tried to introduce a resolution calling for prayer to invoke God's help, gridlock developed in the deliberations of the assembly, and his resolution was discreetly put to one side. The diversity of religious beliefs and the fact that no religious group was clearly dominant made it possible for those assembled at Philadelphia to avoid clashing with one another over religious questions. As a result, what emerged from the Constitutional Convention, according to Edward Humphrey "was the very broadest possible point of view when the question of the politico-religious powers of Congress had to be established."[4] Article VI, Section 3 of the Constitution provides that "no religious test shall ever be required as a qualification to any office or public trust under the United States." The First Amendment to the Constitution guarantees: "Congress shall make no law respecting an establishment of religion, or prohibiting the free exercise thereof."

The doctrine of the separation of the institutions of church and state, however interpreted and implemented, did not separate love of God from love of country. Both were interwoven in the fabric of American life. That the hand of God had guided the American destiny and experience from the very beginning was an important factor in the development of American patriotism.[5] Because of this association of the United State's destiny with the hand of God, according to historian Merle Curti, "the bible figured as a sacred patriotic symbol for the nation."[6]

George Washington well understood the interrelationship between religion and democracy. In his farewell address of September 1796, he gave this advice to the nation: "Of all the dispositions and habits which lead to political prosperity, Religion and Morality are indispensable support. For in vain would that man claim the tribute of patriotism who should labor to subvert these great pillars of human happiness, these firmest props of the duties of men and citizens."[7]

Nor was Washington insensitive to the fact that, though few in number, there were some citizens of the new nation who were not Christians. To the Hebrew Congregation of Newport, Rhode Island, he wrote (1781): "for happily the government of the United States which gives to bigotry no sanction, to persecution no assistance, requires only that they who live under its protection should demean themselves as good citizens in giving it on all occasions their effectual support."[8]

It was a religious movement more than any other that provided the colonies with some semblance of unity, that would stand them in good stead when the War for Independence erupted. That religious movement was the first Great Awakening (1725–50), which in America was led by Jonathan Edwards and the eloquent fire-and-brimstone preacher George Whitefield. These preachers painted a lurid picture of the torments of the sinful and the need for men and women to experience renewed religious zeal. During revival meetings enthralled listeners would loudly tell one and all of their sinfulness, of their conversion, of their renewed religious commitment. And, as tangible evidence of that commitment, they dug deeply into their pockets as the collection plate was passed.

The Great Awakening stimulated a grassroots religious movement that gave strength to ordinary men and women and broke the hold of the upper classes on the church. As a spontaneous mass movement of the American people, it helped break down sectional boundaries on the one hand and religious rigidities on the other. Having wrought a revolution against entrenched clerics, could a revolution against entrenched monarchs be far behind?

Alexis de Tocqueville, a French observer who discerned so much about America when he visited the nation for nine months in 1831–32, grasped the importance of religion in American life. He wrote:

> *There is no country in the world in which the Christian religion retains a greater influence over the souls of men than in America. . . . In the United States religion exercises but little influence upon the laws and upon the details of public opinion but it directs the manners of the community, and by regulating domestic life, it regulates the state. . . . Religion in America takes no direct part in government of society, but it must, nevertheless, be regarded as the foremost of political institutions of the country, for if it does not impart a taste for freedom it facilitates the use of free institutions. This opinion . . . belongs to the whole nation and to every rank of society. I am certain they hold it to be indispensable to the maintenance of republican institutions.*[9]

And James Bryce, a British scholar and diplomat who had a high regard for the U.S. Constitution, wrote:

> *It was religious zeal and the religious conscience which led to the founding of the New England colonies two centuries and a half ago. . . . It is an old saying that monarchies live by honor and republics by virtue. The more democratic republics become, the more the masses grow conscious of their own powers, the more do they need to live, and not only by patriotism, but by reverence and self-control, and the more essential to their well-being are those sources whence a reverence and self-control flow.*[10]

Shailer Mathews, writing in 1918 as World War I ended, summarized his thoughts on the relationship between patriotism and religion:

> *(1) Religion fit for democracy will ennoble patriotism by giving moral direction to the spiritual life of a nation; (2) Religion is needed to strengthen the heart of the patriot in days of national trial; (3) Religion can serve patriotism by freeing it from vindictiveness and personal hatreds; (4) Religion can serve patriotism by furnishing the moral enthusiasm for organizing an international order that shall make nations moral units; (5) Religion must teach patriotism to see that it is better to give justice than fight for rights.*[11]

Separation of church and state did not alienate Americans from religion. On the contrary, it encouraged religious liberty and religious pluralism. Moreover, it meant that above the state was the conscience of the nation embodied in its religious and educational institutions.

American Education and American Patriotism

During the War of 1812, the American flag apparently was flown for the first time over an American schoolhouse at Catamount Hill, Massachusetts. It was not until the Civil War, however, that the practice of flying the flag atop American schools became widespread. Nevertheless, the symbolic joining of the American flag with the American school demonstrates the close ties American education has had with the encouragement, growth, and development of American patriotism

In colonial days nearly all schools were church related, and with American independence the task of inculcating not only love of God but also love of country fell to those schools. Just as the churches supported the new nation, so too did the schools, which encouraged a national unity without which the new nation could not survive. As public schools grew in number and in importance, it was expected that schoolchildren would learn about their country and so be motivated to defend it against those who would attack or undermine it. Love of country and devotion to it would be enhanced if every person knew something of the country's history, especially about the working of American patriots in presiding over the nation's birth. Where else would young Americans learn such famous patriotic sentiments as "Give me liberty or give me death," and "Liberty and Union, now and forever, one and inseparable."

It was the teacher's role to be well acquainted with the history of the country and impart what they knew to their students in such a way that a sense of national unity and support for its ideals would be assured. In 1837, the College of Teachers in Cincinnati voted in favor of making American history a required subject of study in the common schools. They urged, too, that an understanding of the U.S. Constitution be developed, along with an awareness of how the government works, the nature of its laws, and the need for obedience to those laws.

American history textbooks told of the heroic work of the Founding Fathers and spoke of the unique mission of America in bringing liberty and justice to all humankind. In the pages of these textbooks, passages extolled America as the land of opportunity, the cradle of liberty, the home of democracy, the land of the free, and the home of the brave. Civic virtue was exulted, as was the heroism of American soldiers, sailors, and marines. Assembly programs, school plays, inspirational prose, poetry, and music served to reinforce patriotic zeal. All of these activities and materials were designed to make young people proud to be Americans.

It was the task of the school to identify those aspects of language, literature, music, art, government, and in some cases, science and arithmetic, which were or could be recast as distinctively American. Readers, grammars, geographies, and spellers all contained references to the merits of the American form of government as more caring than any other and, therefore, worthy of support. These books, such as Noah Webster's influential spellers, were more than lists of words. Instead, they were thoroughly enriched with patriotic selections. Although there were only 21 million people in the country in 1847, between 1783 and 1847, Webster sold more than 24 million copies of his books. In his dictionary and spellers Webster sought to develop an American English, that is, a distinctive American language, which would systematize and organize customary American vocabulary, spelling, and grammar and thereby help unify the nation by winning acceptance for a common standard usage. By unifying American language and differentiating American English from that imposed upon the colonies by England, national unity and devotion would surely follow. Because of his influence Webster was informally called "Schoolmaster of the Republic."

William Holmes McGuffey's readers were among the most widely used schoolbooks. They did more than teach reading. Instead, they encouraged American patriotism and taught moral lessons in what was right and wrong and how to live virtuously in America. Thousands of children were influenced by selections, such as the following from his *Second Reader*: "Beautiful hands are they that do / Deeds that are noble good and true; / Beautiful feet are they that go / Swiftly to lighten another's woe."

Emma Willard, a feminist and leader in the movement to educate women, wrote *A History of the United States*. In it she pictured America's history as one of simplicity, innocence, and "maiden purity."[12] Jedidiah Morse's *American Geography* did more than describe the mountains, rivers, and other topographical features of the new American nation; it urged westward expansion.

For children of a nation that had yet to find its history and develop a collective memory, historians quickly filled the vacuum. George Bancroft produced a ten-volume American history, which he began in 1834. He took a no-nonsense approach, presenting American history admiringly. America's destiny to lead the nations of the world to new plateaus of freedom and democracy was undeniable, and its place in the family of nations assured and deserved.

And, if American children needed to have heroes and role models, there was no shortage of biographers ready to place America's founders in the pantheon of America's secular saints. The best example is Mason Locke (Parson) Weems's famous biography of George Washington. Weems's best-selling biography of the first president went through many editions, but it was not until the fifth edition that he told the highly unlikely story of how George Washington, as a child, confessed to having chopped down his father's cherry tree. The person that emerges from Weems's life of George Washington is a saintly and flawless, if priggish, character. So deep is the myth that to this day our understanding of America's first president is colored by what Parson Weems wrote almost two hundred years ago.

School played a vital role in Americanizing the immigrant. It was the school's responsibility to teach English to newcomers and to instill in them the ways of American life. The school's task was to furnish immigrants with the skills to enable them to participate effectively as citizens of the American republic and as workers in American industry. The larger purpose and outstanding achievement of American schools was to help boys and girls live in America.

The schools not only taught the nature of American democracy, but they also practiced it themselves. Schools went beyond other institutions in embodying the ideals of American democracy. In the school, opportunity was provided for all, based on merit and accomplishment regardless of race, class, wealth, and power. The schools of America may not have achieved this goal altogether. Native Americans, African-Americans, and the urban and rural poor often fell through the cracks and the "common" school may not have served all children equally effectively. They tried to do so, however, and more than other American institutions, they succeeded in practicing American democracy as they contributed to the development of devotion to country.

The school and the classroom were organized to give students some experience in choosing class and school officers, voting in elections for these posts, editing a school newspaper, and in some cases, handling money that was used by clubs and teams. Through such activities, students formed the habits expected of good citizens; namely, to vote in elections, to become candidates for public office, to listen to more than one

A group of students in the 1950s recite the "Pledge of Allegiance" in their classroom.

point of view, to value free speech and press, to accept the decision of majority rule as determined by the outcome of a secret ballot, and to respect minority rights. Thus, the schools sought to encourage habits of civic virtue and reinforce responsibilities expected of them as citizens of a democratic nation.

In assessing the relationship between American schools and American patriotism, it should be noted that no national system of education developed. Despite efforts to form one, no national university was established. Public schools became the responsibility of each state, and public education became the major responsibility of local governments. And while schools of each state are similar in curriculum and organization, they are governed separately.

"Concorde Hymn," "Old Ironsides," and "The Midnight Ride of Paul Revere" overcome state boundaries and local concerns. "My Country 'Tis of Thee" and "America the Beautiful" ring out loud and clear from the young voices of students across the land, uniting them in bonds that are stronger than local factors that might tend to divide them. Thus, "I pledge allegiance to the flag of the United States of America" is recited in classrooms and assembly halls in public, independent, and parochial schools, from schools located in every remote hamlet and major city, and provides the cement that make a self-governing, self-confident nation possible. Through young eyes and from youthful voices have come what Abraham Lincoln called those "mystic chords of memory, stretching from every battlefield and patriot grave to every living heart and hearthstone." The symbols of American patriotism are communicated by each successive generation across the mountain, "through the prairie, to the ocean white with foam," certain in the conviction that God has blessed America, "our home sweet home."

CASE STUDY:
MULTICULTURALISM

Multiculturalism in the schools, at its best, seeks to broaden U.S. history by showing America with its "warts" as well as with its ideals. It seeks to recognize that by the year 2000 one in three children in the public schools of New York and other urban centers will be minorities, most of whom will have no connection with Europe, the continent from which most Americans came. Multiculturalism seeks to encourage understanding of the diversity of the nation, develop self-esteem among minority children, and recognize that Americans live in a global community rather than in splendid isolation.

Interest in a multicultural curriculum for the schools grew out of an awareness that new immigrants were no longer coming mainly from Europe. In 1965, the Immigration Act passed by Congress opened wide the doors of immigration once again and the number of Hispanics and Asian immigrants grew significantly. Yet the new immigrants, like the ones who came at the end of the 19th and early 20th century, came for similar reasons. They sought economic opportunity and to live in a land free of oppression.

At its extremes, however, multiculturalism threatens the unity of America. Multiculturalism goes too far when how we differ is made to seem greater than what we have in common. Stressing the differences between the older immigrants and the new immigrants and preferring ethnic rights to individual rights, liberties, and opportunities is a danger to the unity of the nation.

In too many countries—from the former Soviet Union to the former Yugoslavia, India, Ethiopia, Sri Lanka, Myanmar, Indonesia, Iraq, Cyprus, Nigeria, Angola, Rwanda, Lebanon, Guyana, and Trinidad—ethnic tensions are destroying the fabric of society. Even nations with long histories—such as Britain, France, Belgium, and Spain—are torn by ethnic divisiveness.

The threat of disunion is very real if schools abandon their traditional role of helping to identify what we share in common rather than what drives us apart.

According to the historian Arthur Schlesinger Jr., "The point of America was not to preserve old cultures but to forge a new American culture."[13] To the extent that multiculturalism continues the American tradition of seeking unifying ideals and a common culture, it is a helpful contribution to America. To the extent that the flames of racial and ethnic antagonisms are fanned, it is a threat to the unity of America. When immigration to America was at its height, President Theodore Roosevelt declared, "The one absolutely certain way of bringing this nation to ruin, of preventing all possibility of its being a nation at all, would be to permit it to become a tangle of squabbling nationalities."[14] America is now a more diverse land than it was in Roosevelt's day, yet what he said then is true even today.

American Economy and American Patriotism

Although America is a spiritual nation, it is more commonly thought of as a materialistic one. The ever-practical George Washington, observing the behavior of his "summer soldiers and sunshine patriots," was quick to note that patriotism was not enough. "A great and lasting war," he said, "can never be supported on the principle [of patriotism] alone. It must be aided by the prospect of interest or some reward. For a time, it may, of itself push men to action; to bear much to encounter difficulties; but it will not endure unassisted by interest."[15]

An economic interest that was a pillar of American patriotism was the availability of free land. Merle Curti observed, "Nothing played a more significant role in the development of loyalty to the national government . . . [than] the free homestead."[16] It was the ready availability of free or low-cost land that helped in a very practical and materialistic sense to bind the people of the nation together. Free land, unavailable in the countries from which the colonists had come, confirmed the belief Americans had a national destiny to lead the way to a more prosperous world.

When the early colonists began to feel at home in the New World, they became aware of their continent's vastness, great beauty, and spectacular abundance. They grew to love its substantial forests, turbulent rivers, great plains, and majestic mountains. The very geographic features of the New World evoked the awe and devotion of the early settlers and all who came after them.

The new nation was the largest in the Western world. But its sheer size was a danger as well as an opportunity. There was a danger that a land of such size could not be held together by common ties and was, perhaps, not even governable. Without a monarch to evoke national authority could a government based on republican principles rule a vast domain? On the other hand, there was the opportunity that a land of continental proportions could make relative abundance for large numbers of Americans a reality. In the Old World, people had to eke out a living from a reluctant land and scrimp and save to make meager resources last, but in America nature could be generous with its bounty and materially enrich the lives of all. Here the affluence of the few need not be supported on the backs of the many. Instead, there was opportunity for all to prosper. According to historian Russell Nye, "The nation everywhere . . . was coming then, to be identified with the realization of the American dream of universal enjoyment of the goods of this world."[17]

This illustration shows a panoramic view of New York City in 1768. The abundance of free land in the colonies helped forge a national identity in America.

John Quincy Adams, who later followed in his father's footsteps and become president of the United States, was but 16 years old when he witnessed the signing of the Treaty of Paris (1783), which recognized the independence of the United States. He was an old man, serving in Congress, when California sought admission to the Union. Within a single lifetime the

United States had grown from sea to shining sea. Even in those early days, before the term had been coined, there seemed to be an awareness that the colonists had a manifest destiny to build upon and cultivate the wilderness, to spread over its entire extent, wherever that should ultimately prove to be, and to show the way to a better world. But what kept this large and growing country from fragmenting? Though the land was vast, its rivers were navigable, which reduced, but by no means eliminated, the isolation of the frontier. Later, improved roads and canals made possible the development of a communications network of postal facilities and newspapers, thus linking the eastern seaboard with the western lands. Colonial Americans became aware of one another, of their common problems, and of their common destiny. "The growing interdependence of the sections . . . provided a powerful cohesive force in the development of loyalty to the nation."[18] It made possible a healthy optimism that Americans would prosper.

When the members of the Constitutional Convention sought to break the monotony of their deliberations, they left their meeting place in Philadelphia to watch as John Fitch demonstrated the invention of the age—a steamboat. The industrial revolution, the beginning of which paralleled the birth of the United States, provided the technical means by which the vastness of America could be conquered. Within fifty years, the nation was tied together with a network of canals, roads, and later railroads. America's size would prove to be an asset, not a liability, as some had feared.

Regionalism did appear as first New England and later the Confederacy sought to break away. It took a victory over England in 1812 to remove the threat of disunity in New England and the bloodiest of wars to return the Confederacy to the Union. But the historian Henry Steele Commager reminds us that "American patriotism is associated with the whole of the American territory rather than with particular places. . . . While in the Old World it is the locality that inspires loyalty and patriotism, in the New it is the whole country."[19]

THE EMERGENCE OF THE AMERICAN

The colonists shared a common knowledge that they were unlikely ever to return to their former homelands. Although some people went back, most did not have the money to buy passage to recross the sea. For the most part, those who came to these shores had come to stay, to settle, and to raise their families.

American religion, education, economy, and geography all helped to create a new person, the American. Although the English tradition was dominant, by 1776 there were colonists from other countries who had different points of origin, different roots and customs, and who spoke languages other than English. But both English and non-English colonists felt dwindling ties to the English crown. The ceremonial offices of the royal governors, still filled with the pomp and ceremony characteristic of monarchy, soon seemed empty of meaning in the more informal environment of the New World. By the time of the Declaration of Independence the colonists were ready to forgo the homage due royalty and were prepared to challenge the king.

A distinctive "American," however, was slow in emerging. Originally, all the colonists who came from England viewed themselves as simply English men and women who lived in America. Later on, perhaps as early as 1691, the Reverend Cotton Mather used the term "American" to identify those English people who lived in the New World. By the early eighteenth century, "American" was used in Europe to ridicule the yokels who lived in the new land. Benjamin Franklin declared that to Europeans, "American" was still understood "to be a kind of Yahoo."[20] However, even at that late date, the term "American" was not generally associated with a person of any less loyalty to the British crown. In 1776 Patrick Henry, somewhat carried away with his oratory, declared to the Continental Congress in Williamsburg, Virginia, "I am not a Virginian, but an American." Although Patrick Henry's words did not make it so, the American as a distinctive type was gradually emerging.

The Declaration of Independence clearly united the thirteen colonies against Britain. On September 9, 1776, the Continental Congress declared that "the United States" would replace the "United Colonies" on all commissions and official documents issued under the authority of Congress.

At the Constitutional Convention, Charles C. Pinckney advised his colleagues that Americans were neither English, nor European, nor Greek, nor Roman. The people of the country were, he said, a distinctive people. Therefore, he declared, the convention must think and plan for the growth of "a new country." On May 3, 1787, the Constitutional Convention adopted a resolution declaring that "a national government ought to be established." Despite this resolution, however, nowhere is the term "national" used in the U.S. Constitution.

Local loyalties remained strong, and devotion to the nation was slow in fixing itself in the minds of ordinary people. They were fretful that the new government might take from the people the liberties they had wrested from the crown. Nevertheless, by the time the U.S. Constitution was adopted, there did emerge a new person—an American. In his *Letters from an American Farmer*, Michel-Guillaume Jean de Crèvecoeur asked: "What then is the American this new Man?" In answering his own question Crèvecoeur concluded: "He is an American, who leaving behind all his ancient prejudices and manners receives new ones from the new mode of life he has embraced, the new government he obeys, and the new rank he holds. . . . Here individuals of all nations are melted into a new race of men."[21]

In due course, Americans from every walk of life, the original settler, the new immigrant, even the enslaved, and later the freeman and freewoman, came to accept with greater or lesser intensity a set of values or goals to which the nation as a whole aspired. It was thought that the American Creed, as this came to be called, when perfected would lead to the creation of the "heavenly city" that John Winthrop envisioned. What then is the nature of the American Creed? What are its essential principles? How carefully had the nation committed itself to them and their accomplishment? How did it contribute to American patriotism?

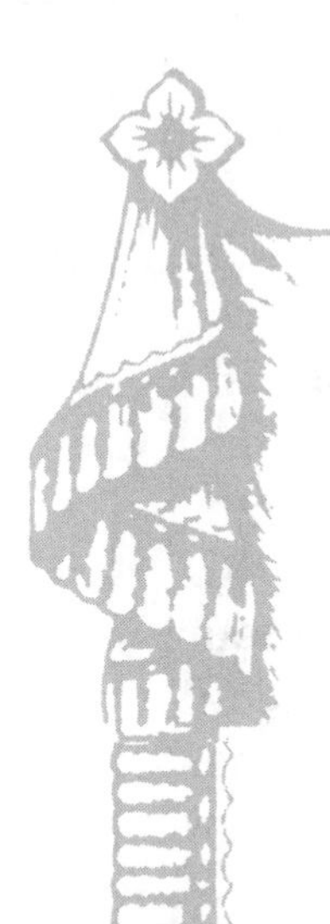

THREE

PATRIOTISM AND THE AMERICAN CREED

Democracy will not come
Today, this year
Nor ever
Through compromise and fear.[1]
—Langston Hughes,
poet

Toward the end of World War I a contest was held in which the participants were invited to write the briefest possible summary of America's ideals, of what the country stands for, as revealed in its history and traditions and as expressed in the words of its great documents and great leaders. The mayor of Baltimore offered a prize of $1,000 for the winning statement in the belief that it was appropriate for the city that was the birthplace of "The Star-Spangled Banner" to do this. The successful statement was written by William Tyler Page, whose family had come to America in 1650 and had settled in Williamsburg, Virginia. The American Creed, as the statement came to be called, was inscribed in the *Congressional Record* on April 11, 1918. In one hundred words William Tyler Page summed up America's political ideals:

> *I believe in the United States of America as a Government of the people, by the people, for the people; whose just powers are derived from the consent of the governed; a democracy in a republic; a sovereign Nation of many sovereign States; a perfect union, one and inseparable; established upon those principles of freedom, equality, justice, and humanity for which American patriots sacrificed their lives and fortunes. I therefore believe it is my duty to my country to love it, to support its Constitution, to obey its laws, to respect its flag, and to defend it against all enemies.*

In our day a common core of ideals which may be called the American Creed consists of those essential beliefs that Americans hold dear. Although patriotism in general has been defined as the love of the land where one lives and to which one gives allegiance, in America the ideals to which America gave birth have been more important in helping Americans think of themselves as a nation.

These ideals have been accepted by rich and poor, by men and women of every race and religion in every section of the country. Ralph Bunche, a distinguished African-American political scientist and diplomat, wrote: "Every man [and woman], white, black, red or yellow knows that this is the 'land of the free,' the 'land of opportunity,' the 'cradle of liberty,' the 'home of democracy,' that the American flag symbolizes the 'equality of all men [and women],' and guarantees to all 'the protection of life, liberty and property,' freedom of speech, freedom of religion, and racial tolerance."[2]

THE LAND OF THE FREE

America is the world's first new nation. It was the first major colony to break away successfully from colonial rule through revolution. America set an example of how a colonial people might free itself from the grip of an imperial power. Those who as Ralph Waldo Emerson put it "fired the shot heard 'round the world" were, in effect, setting an example that is still followed today by people of other countries who seek to establish a nation within secure borders where they can observe their own laws, customs, and traditions. During nearly all of America's history, by its example, words, and deeds, America has encouraged oppressed people to seek freedom through peaceful means if possible, through revolution if necessary.

It was to this land of the free that the Puritans, the Pilgrims, and religious dissenters of nearly every belief came in hopes of finding the freedom to worship as they preferred. It was to the land of the free that immigrants from every continent come to escape the tyranny of oppression and to enjoy the benefits of a free-market economy. It was in the land of the free that the Mayflower Compact, the first constitution, was written, enabling the people of Plymouth to "frame just and equal Laws, Ordinances, Acts, Constitutions, and Offices from time to time as shall be thought most meet and convenient for the general Good of the colony." It was also in the land of the free that the Philadelphia lawyer Andrew Hamilton defended John Peter Zenger, a New York newspaper publisher who was accused of libel (writing falsely about another person). Zenger was held in prison for nine months for criticizing the royal governor of New York. Hamilton eloquently insisted that he was not merely defending a poor printer but was speaking on behalf of every person who lived in the American colonies. "It is the Best Cause," he declared. "It is the cause of liberty." He went on to insist that speaking and writing the truth could not be considered libelous.

The Land of Opportunity

To James Russell Lowell, a prominent 19th-century writer and diplomat, the very essence of democracy was equal opportunity. He described democracy as "that form of society in which every man [and woman] has a chance and knows that he has it." And Abraham Lincoln spoke to the question of America as a land of opportunity in these words: "We proposed [in the Declaration of Independence] to give all a chance, and we expected the weak to grow stronger; the ignorant, wiser; and all better and happier together."

The common, or public, school was to be the chief instrument by which the country encouraged the idea of providing equal opportunity for all its people. This was in Jefferson's mind when he drafted his early proposals for free public education in Virginia. Horace Mann, the driving force behind public education, called the common school "the balance wheel" of the republic. Common schools would teach the three Rs—reading, 'riting, and 'rithmetic—to the illiterate, along with industrial techniques and factory discipline to the unskilled, thereby enabling the less affluent to have the opportunity to earn more of the nation's wealth. The common school was to Americanize immigrants by helping them learn English and by teaching them the traditions of their adopted land. For example, Mary Antin, a Russian-born immigrant, found the public schools of Boston entirely open to her, "no application made, no questions asked, no examinations, rulings, exclusions; no machinations, no fees. The door stood open to every one of us."[3]

Although one can identify those who are America's first families and those who move in centers of political and economic power, Americans perceive theirs to be a land in which they, their children, or their children's children may one day be among those who wield political power. From Benjamin Franklin to President Bill Clinton, America as a land of opportunity has been an essential part of the American Creed.

THE CRADLE OF LIBERTY

Among the inalienable rights of Americans is "the right to life, liberty, and the pursuit of happiness." These self-evident truths of the Declaration of Independence were to be embodied in a more formal document, the U.S. Constitution. That document was described by the British prime minister William Gladstone as "the most wonderful work ever struck off at a given time by the brain and purpose of man." When it was written, the U.S. Constitution was the most democratic document in the world. No other provided so much opportunity for the expression of liberty. By the cradle of liberty Americans primarily mean the right to worship, speak, read, and write as they wish. They mean the right to be protected from being required to testify against themselves, the rights of privacy, and the right to be left alone in pursuit of

Delegates to the Constitutional Convention await their turn to sign the U.S. Constitution. The document guarantees the rights of American citizens.

their lawful activities. This was particularly true in the safeguards to liberty established in the Bill of Rights, the first ten amendments to the Constitution.

The U.S. Constitution provides for a government of laws, not of men. It builds in safeguards that have prevented one branch of government—Congress, the president, or the Supreme Court—from becoming too powerful over too long a period of time. It is a government of limited powers, that is, what the government may do is explicitly stated in the Constitution. Although it has been interpreted and reinterpreted through usage, amendment, and legislation to meet the needs of a modern nation, what is remarkable about the Constitution is that it has lasted so long as the law of the land.

As the cradle of liberty, the American Creed held that America was destined to teach the meaning of liberty throughout the world. For example, Alexander Hamilton, a leader during the American Revolution and our first secretary of the treasury, believed that the American Revolution had penetrated the "gloomy regions of despotism" that were found in Europe. Thomas Jefferson's secretary of the treasury, Albert Gallatin, a Swedish immigrant, believed that his adopted country would "be a model republic" whose example would improve the world's condition. This aspect of the American Creed took on a religious zeal in that many Americans held that God had established the new republic precisely to bring enlightenment to the nations of the world.

The Home of Democracy

America, as the home of democracy, is based on the constitutional provision that calls for government by consent of the governed. The American Creed places its confidence in local, state, and national institutions through which justice is achieved, liberty encouraged, and order established. In writing the Constitution, the founders believed that the republic they created in 1787 would become the democracy of today. Living in the home of democracy, Americans have placed their confidence in majority rule with respect for minority rights. That the ballot, not the bullet, was the appropriate way by which wrongs can be righted and reforms achieved has long been a vital part of the American Creed. John Greenleaf Whittier, one of America's prominent poets of American patriotism, put the matter this way in his poem "The Poor Voter on Election Day": "While there's a right to need my vote / A wrong to sweep away, / Up clouted knee and ragged coat! / A man's a man today!"

When President Woodrow Wilson sought to justify American participation in World War I, he used the slogan, "The world must be made safe for democracy." These words struck a responsive chord with the American public; during the war years, at least, most Americans agreed with them. Wilson believed American democracy to be the norm of democracy everywhere and anywhere. He saw the war, and wanted Americans to see the war, as a logical extension of their own inclination to view themselves as a model of democratic form and practice that the other nations of the world would eagerly copy. The Wilsonian democratic ideal was "the Americanization of the world."[4]

Equality for All

That "all men are created equal" is, of course, derived directly from the Declaration of Independence. It is not altogether clear exactly what the Founding Fathers meant by this statement. But the ideal of equality was one about which there was little disagreement. The founders of the republic believed that in America there were fewer class differences and fewer distinctions based on birth, wealth, or social class than in any other country in history. James Madison informed members of the Constitutional Convention that Americans had "fewer distinctions of fortune and less of rank" than was the case anywhere else.

In 1857, in a speech at Springfield, Illinois, Abraham Lincoln attempted to interpret what the nation's founders might have meant by equality:

> *I think the authors of that notable instrument [the Declaration of Independence] intended to include all men, but they did not intend to declare all men equal in all respects. They did not mean to say all were equal in color, size, intellect, moral development, or social capacity. They defined with tolerable distinctness in what respects they did consider all men created equal—equal with "certain inalienable rights, among which are life, liberty, and the pursuit of happiness." This they said and this they meant. They did not mean to assert the obvious untruth that all were then actually enjoying that equality, nor yet that they were about to confer it immediately upon them. In fact, they had no power to confer such a boon. They meant simply to declare the right, so that enforcement of it might follow as fast as circumstances would permit.*

Although Jefferson recognized an aristocracy of talent and of virtue as opposed to an aristocracy of birth or of wealth, President Andrew Jackson ushered in the era of the "common man." Jacksonian democracy, as it is called, holds that any person has the talent to serve in government, to take part in the affairs of state, and to hold public office. It was under Jackson that the so-called spoils system was introduced, whereby the victorious political party would enjoy the spoils of their victory by ousting the appointees of the previous administration and by putting into office, by way of reward, new officials who, being the equal of others, could perform any assignment equally well.

The existence of a frontier likewise encouraged an emphasis on equality. In the wilderness men and

Case Study: Colonial Williamsburg

From 1699 to 1779 Williamsburg, Virginia, was the seat of government for Great Britain's largest colony. Here, the House of Burgesses, the first elected representative body in colonial America, met during those fateful years leading to the American Revolution. When the government was in session this village of two thousand expanded to as many as six thousand men and women and thus, in colonial terms, was an important metropolis.

In 1779, however, fearful that Williamsburg might be threatened by British forces and aware of the need for a more central location, the seat of government was moved to Richmond. With the government no longer present, Williamsburg became a college town (the College of William and Mary). While it remained, for a time, the scene of lively Fourth of July celebrations, it was not long before the town began to stagnate. In 1928, however, John D. Rockefeller Jr. undertook the financing of the restoration of Williamsburg to how it was when the oratory of Washington, Jefferson, Patrick Henry, and others filled the air. He expected that once the national memory had been prodded, the patriotism of Americans would likewise be encouraged.

But in such historic restorations, what should be restored? Rockefeller gradually began acquiring important real estate. A distinguished historical advisory committee was established to identify the precise location of the historic Duke of Gloucester Street and the historic buildings including the palace of the royal governor, the House of Burgesses, Raleigh Tavern, even the jail. An equally prominent architectural firm was engaged to restore the buildings in the most authentic detail possible. But in the process of acquiring the land, restoring the buildings, and staffing them with costumed representatives of the times, a number of paradoxes developed.

Although the Rockefeller family had a long-standing tradition of trying to improve the education of African-Americans, in the process of restoring Colonial Williamsburg many homes and community institutions of blacks were destroyed, thereby exacerbating race relationships. Because Colonial Williamsburg was being restored during a time when racial segregation still ruled, a separate dormitory was built for African-American workers. Thus, those attempting to restore a symbol of liberty bowed to the dictates of the region and custom of the times and so contributed to racial segregation.

Initially, only a sanitized version of Colonial Williamsburg was offered. Although the men in the Virginia House of Burgesses spoke of freedom, liberty, and revolution, most of them were slave owners. That the Williamsburg of colonial days was a society that rested on slavery was at first almost totally ignored. Should the hovels of the slave quarters be restored? Would visitors really want to see this seamy side of America's past?

Nor were men and women of color welcome at any of the grand hotels that were built to accommodate a growing number of visitors to the site. Separate restroom facilities were established, and in restored Colonial Williamsburg African-Americans could scarcely get something to eat let alone a place to sleep. Jews were also discriminated against. Few, if any, Jews served on any of the governing boards of Colonial Williamsburg. Discrimination against Jews who sought accommodations at the elegant Williamsburg Inn was widespread and consistent.

Colonial Williamsburg is a national treasure and the forerunner of other restorations designed both to demonstrate how our forebears lived and to stroke American patriotism. But in these restorations should one show only the best of the past or also the shameful side of far off days? Today, we have become more sophisticated about what we restore and how best to do it. We are more likely to emphasize the reality of the times with warts and all rather than offering a sanitized version of how we would like to believe our forebears behaved. In a sense such restorations are a microcosm of American society as a whole. How do we square the American conscience, which recognizes our shortcomings, with the standards established in the American Creed?

---

women faced equal danger from tempestuous weather and predatory animals. They risked death from famine, illness, or hostile Indians who were losing their lands as the frontier moved. Differences in wealth and certainly of birth were not extreme. There was an expression on the frontier that "a fool can sometimes put on his coat better than a wise man can do it for him."

This view summed up the egalitarian tendency of the day, including the concepts of one person one vote, equality before the law, justice impartially administered through a jury of one's peers, procedural safeguards to be identical for all. All these remain part of the American Creed.

The American Creed and the American Conscience

One cannot deny that sometimes only lip service has been paid to the American Creed. For some, America has not been a land of the free, nor the home of democracy, nor the land of opportunity. Slavery existed for two hundred years before the Emancipation Proclamation of 1863, a handicap with which the nation was born, and its ravages have not yet been overcome in the nation's maturity. When the Declaration of Independence and the Constitution were written, enslaved men, women, and children worked as field hands, household servants, and occasionally in mines and factories. Enslaved people were considered property rather than people and, as property, could be bought and sold.

The rights of women were likewise essentially ignored despite Abigail Adams urging her husband John to "remember the ladies." The Constitution left the determination of who may be eligible to vote to the states, and so initially, voting was largely in the hands of white male property owners. In recognizing the inequality of voting privileges, Thomas Jefferson urged that each white man who had less than fifty acres be given at least this minimum amount.

Equality of opportunity for all has not yet been achieved. Disagreements have sometimes turned into violence and confrontation, and order has not always been preserved. Free speech and press have sometimes been denied, and privacy has sometimes been invaded. As new technologies such as interactive television, computer-assisted telecommunications, voice mail, and the like become more widespread, we have yet to wrestle with the implications of the new communications media for freedom of expression.

Minorities and women have had to struggle to be included in the promises of the American Creed, and immigrants have not always been welcome on these shores. Jury trial and procedural safeguards have not always been fairly applied, and on occasion, the rights of wealth, property, or privilege have placed obstacles in the way of expressing the wishes of the people. Some people have sought to impose white, Anglo-Saxon "superiority" on America and have resorted to hooded terrorism to impose their own, distorted brand of patriotism.

The religious liberty and search for diversity that propelled the early colonists westward and that the Founding Fathers safeguarded in the Constitution have, at times, been threatened. Some groups have, for example, attempted to make it difficult, dangerous, or uncomfortable for Jews to practice their religion, and others have sought to restrict the freedom of worship of Roman Catholics. The Mormons had to overcome intense hostility before they could gain acceptance into the mainstream of American society.

It has been especially difficult for African-Americans to free themselves from being the victims of discriminatory practices. Poll taxes limited their right to vote. Bigotry limited where they could live and work. Yet, as Martin Luther King Jr. reminded his congregation when he first took to the pulpit of the Dexter Avenue Baptist Church in Montgomery, Alabama:

> *There comes a time when people get tired of being trampled over by the iron fist of oppression. . . . We are here because we are tired now. . . . The only weapon we have in our hands this evening is the weapon of protest. If we were incarcerated behind the iron curtains of a communist nation—we couldn't do this. If we were trapped in the dungeon of a totalitarian regime—we couldn't do this. But the great glory of American democracy is the right to protest for right.*

And, on August 28, 1963, before 250,000 people who had marched on Washington, D.C., he declared: "I have a dream that one day the nation will rise up and live out the true meaning of its creed . . . all men are created equal."

There is a built-in conflict between America as a land of opportunity and America as a land of equality. Equality and opportunity are ideas that clash with one another. One person's opportunity to gain wealth or power may sometimes be realized only at the expense of another's desire to be equal. Indeed, much of America's history may be interpreted in terms of how Americans have sought to resolve these conflicting ideals.

Clearly, Americans have sometimes fallen short of the American Creed. Nevertheless, the American Creed establishes a norm against which to measure the extent to which Americans have lived up to these ideals. American patriotism is not unquestioned loyalty to a great leader, to a political party, or to a venerated soil. It is a commitment to a basic set of ideals and values that help define America and what it aspires to be. Lincoln said it best when he spoke of the writers of the Declaration of Independence: "They meant to set up a standard maxim for a free society, which could be familiar to all, and revered by all; constantly looked to, constantly approximated, and thereby constantly spreading and deepening its influence, and augmenting the happiness and value of life to all people of all colors everywhere." American heroes, among them Abraham Lincoln and Martin Luther King Jr., are those who cling to the American Creed and strive to achieve its ideals.

The Home of the Brave

American patriotism has been nurtured by the heroic deeds of brave men and women who have come to symbolize those ideals for which America stands. Clearly, the founders of the republic and Abraham Lincoln are among the first rank of America's heroes. Louisa May Alcott and Elizabeth Cady Stanton are among America's heroes for the courage they demonstrated fighting for the rights of women against enormous odds and against the prevailing temper of the times. Other heroes include: Harriet Beecher Stowe, for her novel *Uncle Tom's Cabin*, which drove home

On August 28, 1963, thousands of demonstrators crowd the Mall in Washington D.C. during the March on Washington. The march was held to demand equal rights for African-Americans.

the evils of slavery to those who had yet to be convinced; Helen Keller, for the example she set of courage and fortitude in her fight to overcome her inability to hear, see, or speak; Frederick Douglass, Booker T. Washington, W. E. B. Du Bois, and Martin Luther King Jr., all of whom who sought to improve the lives of African-Americans.

Those who showed bravery in combat are heroes: Nathan Hale, Colonel William Prescott, John Paul Jones, and Molly Pitcher, who supplied the troops with water at the Battle of Monmouth and then, at least according to legend, took up the cannon that fell from the hands of her fatally wounded husband. Each war and each crisis gives birth to a new crop of heroes: Andrew Jackson, the victor at the Battle of New Orleans during the War of 1812; Union generals Ulysses S. Grant and William T. Sherman and Confederate generals Robert E. Lee and Thomas (Stonewall) Jackson of the Civil War; Theodore Roosevelt, who led the charge at the Battle of San Juan Hill in Cuba; Sergeant Alvin York, World War I's most celebrated soldier; and World War II generals Dwight D. Eisenhower, Douglas MacArthur, and George C. Marshall.

The list of American heroes is long. Heroes of either sex and of every race have not only contributed to the well-being of the nation but have also demonstrated through their deeds their own patriotism, thereby setting an example of devotion and self-sacrifice. We pay homage to them because, as Dixon Wecter wrote, "homage to heroes is a vital part of our patriotism."[5] Heroes become for us symbols of what we are, what we were, and what we aspire to be. Let us examine the symbols by which we have sought to remind Americans of their past and of what Americans hope for the future.

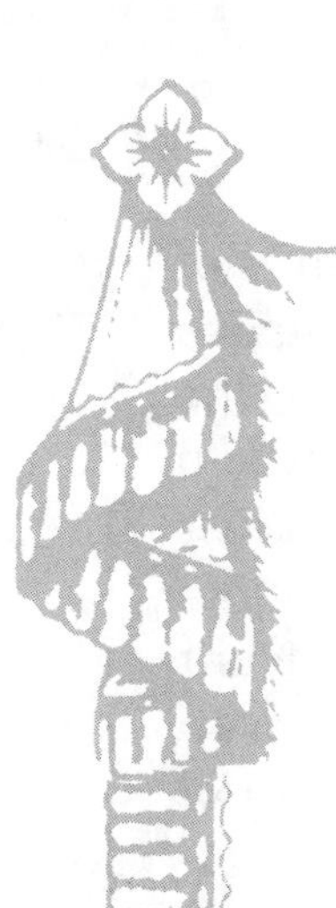

Four

Symbols of American Patriotism

Let me be a free man—free to work, free to trade, free to choose my teachers, free to follow the religion of my fathers, free to talk for myself and I will obey every law, or submit to the penalty.

— Chief Joseph of the Nez Percé, 1879

"The United States began its existence," Russell Nye reminds us, "with none of the symbolic equipment—heroes, legends, flags, monuments, and so on—needed to express and demonstrate national feeling."[1] Francis Grund, a European who traveled in the United States during the Jacksonian period (1829–37), understood that American patriotism was based on equality of expectation, the unifying force of American religious institutions, and the American conviction that the nation had a moral commitment to lead the world toward a better future.[2] But having rebelled against the Crown and against all the symbolism and ceremonialism that the court of England inspired, what symbols would enlist the enthusiasm of the American people for the new nation and rally them in support of these revolutionary ideals? What symbols would capture the ideas upon which the new nation was built and cultivate patriotism in a nation so recently established?

In their longing for appropriate symbols representative of the ideals of the new nation, early generations of Americans tended to draw on ancient Israel, Greece, and Rome. As a republic it seemed natural for the United States to look, in particular, to the ancient Roman republic for direction. As a democracy it seemed fitting that the nation would look to Greece, especially to ancient Athens, for vision. As a people who had made an exodus from Europe, it seemed appropriate that for certain purposes the experiences of the ancient Hebrews, who made an exodus from Egypt, would serve as a source for symbolic inspiration.

One by one, in a gradual process, patriotic symbolism in the United States developed as a matter of necessity rather than of urgency, and in a real sense, American patriotic symbolism may be said to be evolving still. Some patriotic symbols developed spontaneously as Americans became aware that they were becoming a different people in that they were casting off the qualities and characteristics of the lands from which they had come.

Brother Jonathan, Uncle Sam, and Yankee Doodle

The symbols Brother Jonathan, Yankee Doodle, and Uncle Sam are intimately interwoven. Today, the symbol of Brother Jonathan has disappeared, while those of Yankee Doodle and Uncle Sam stand collectively for the American people, their government, and the nation's mission.

Brother Jonathan and Yankee Doodle were used by the British and by those Americans loyal to the Crown to poke fun at the American patriots who were fighting John Bull (the symbol of the British people) for their freedom and independence. Brother Jonathan was frequently thought of as the son of John Bull.

The origins of Brother Jonathan and Yankee Doodle are obscure. Though originally intended as a mild insult, they were taken up by colonial Americans to denote American virtues of courage, optimism, informality, shrewdness, and candor. George Washington frequently used the term "Brother Jonathan" when referring to his troops. He is believed to have frequently said, "We must consult Brother Jonathan." Just whom he meant is not always clear. But if he did not mean "we must see how the soldiers feel," it may have been a reference to Governor Jonathan Trumbull of Connecticut, a man whose counsel General Washington often found helpful.

The term "Brother Jonathan" survived the Revolution. As the threat from Europe grew and the War of 1812 drew nearer, patriotic plays and songs often referred to the stalwart Brother Jonathan, and the term was used with increasing frequency, often times interchangeably with Yankee, as the following excerpt from an 1808 play indicates:

This illustration shows John Bull (Great Britain) facing off against Brother Jonathan (the United States).

Then Jonathan and I went down
To look around the wharf, Sir,
And there we see a hundred men
Shoving a big boat off, Sir.
Yankee Doodle keep it up,
Yankee Doodle Dandy,
We'll soak our hides in home-made rum,
If we can't get French Brandy.

The reference here is to the fact that the British were interfering with American shipping and some imported products were not reaching the United States.

But if we do not know precisely who Brother Jonathan was, we do have some idea as to the qualities he was supposed to have possessed. Jonathan, the younger son of John Bull, was settled on some new land that his father urged him to cultivate as his portion of the family inheritance:

In a little time Jonathan grew up to be very large for his age; and became a tall, stout, double-jointed, broadfooted cub of a fellow, awkward in his gait, and simple in his appearance; but shewing a lively, shrewd look, and having the promise of great strength when he should get to his full growth. He was rather an odd looking chap . . . and he was apt to be blustering and saucy, but in the main he was a peaceable sort of careless fellow, that would quarrel with nobody if you only let him alone. He used to dress in homespun trousers with a huge bagging seat, which seemed to have nothing in it. This made people say he had no bottom; whoever said so lied, as they found to their cost, whenever they put Jonathan in a passion. He always wore a short Linsey-woolsey coat, that did not above half cover his breech, and the sleeves of which were so short and his hand and wrist came out beyond them, looking like a shoulder of mutton. All which was in consequence of his growing so fast that he outgrew his clothes.[3]

Thus, Brother Jonathan was viewed as a kind of country bumpkin, awkward in movement, odd in appearance, yet with it all, good-hearted, somewhat shrewd, slow to anger, simple, thrifty, courageous, good-natured, and tolerant. These were among the attributes that some thought reasonably reflected the American character of those days.

As Brother Jonathan grew up, he proved to be too simple for the emerging industrial nation whose people had fought England in what some called a second War for Independence (War of 1812). A more sophisticated character was needed, so Brother Jonathan blended into Yank, Yankee, or Yankee Doodle. In 1865 Colonel James F. Rusling wrote, "Brother Jonathan is dead. Born in another age, and of the day of small things, he has passed away. His name, even bids fair to become myth among the people. . . . Today the true representative American is the Union soldier. Yankee Doodle is decidedly looking up."[4]

To Europeans, the term "Yank" generally referred to the soldiers sent to Europe during World War I while the term "Yankee" was a more general, if colloquial, synonym for American. In the United States, however, the term has often been confined to the native population of New England, to the peddlers who left the barren farms of Vermont, Maine, and New Hampshire and took their Yankee notions (pins, scarves, rings, fabric, hairpins, thread, needles, etc.) to supply rural and frontier people with goods they could not easily obtain. The Yankee peddler earned a reputation, sometimes merited sometimes not, of being a shrewd merchant who bore watching lest he swindle the sturdy people of the frontier with his ingenuity and lack of integrity.

Unlike Brother Jonathan and Yankee Doodle, the term Uncle Sam refers not so much to the people as it does to the government. Thus, a government worker might well say, "I work for Uncle Sam," meaning the federal government of the United States. The qualities ascribed to Uncle Sam are similar to, but not exactly identical with, those associated with Brother Jonathan. Merle Curti notes, "Uncle Sam, while primarily the symbol of the federal government, also resembled the qualities ascribed to the American people . . . courage, thrift, simplicity, an ability to carry more than a fair share of the load, a capacity to labor and to make lightning decisions, and an optimism not to be floored."[5] It was not until the Civil War that a cartoon figure we know of Uncle Sam became generally familiar to Americans through the illustrations of Thomas Nast.

The emergence of Uncle Sam as an affectionate name for the American government may have taken initial shape during the War of 1812. According to one story, Sam Wilson and his brother Ebenezer were prominent merchants in the meatpacking business in the city of Troy, New York, and supplied American troops during the War of 1812. In time, the two became the chief suppliers to Elbert Anderson, the head purchaser of meat for the American troops in the area.

When a group of visitors, including the governor, visited the Wilson meatpacking plant they saw meat stamped "E.A.U.S." Upon inquiring of a nearby workman, they learned that E.A. stood for Elbert Anderson, and the workman quipped, "U.S. was for Uncle Sam," that is, for "Uncle Sam" Wilson. Of course, the letters actually meant "United States." The nickname caught on quickly and before long the products supplied by Sam Wilson, those supplied by others, and even the troops who used them were called "Uncle Sams," much as the term "G.I." (for "government issue") came to be applied to American soldiers during World War II.

In time the city of Troy was officially identified as the original home of Uncle Sam. The Boy Scouts of the area still tend to the grave of Sam Wilson by ensuring that only flags that have flown over the White House are flown over his grave. September 13 was designated by then governor of New York Nelson Rockefeller, as "Uncle Sam Day." In 1961, Congress adopted a resolution saluting Uncle Sam Wilson as "the progenitor of the American national symbol."[6]

Some people believe that, just as Brother Jonathan disappeared from the scene as an appropriate symbol of the American people, this same fate also awaits Uncle Sam. The historian Allen Nevins said: "His world is gone. He seems to carry too much Yankee cuteness. . . . What's more, Uncle Sam lends himself too easily to ludicrous or sinister caricature in other lands."[7] Whether or not this is so remains to be seen. Although some symbols of America change as the nation ages and matures, others, developed in the early days of the republic, endure to prod the national memory, to provide a bridge between the past and the present, and to reflect on the nation's future. Let us see what some of these symbols are.

The Great Seal

In the beginning Americans were reluctant to abandon altogether those symbolic ties with England that were so charged with sentiment and pageantry. Yet once having cut the ties with that country, developing new symbols became necessary. Such symbols would not only cultivate American patriotism but would help the nation go about its business. For example, a national seal had to be created to express concretely the fact of American independence. This seal would appear on all official and formal documents of the new United States. What should it look like? Who should take responsibility for its creation?

A committee consisting of Benjamin Franklin, Thomas Jefferson, and John Adams devoted some of its time to the design of the Great Seal of the United States. In 1776 Franklin proposed that the Great Seal consist of an image of Moses leading the children of Israel out of Egyptian bondage. Jefferson thought the Great Seal should show the ancient Hebrew exodus from Egypt through the wilderness to the promised land. Though not adopted, these symbolic representations indicate clearly that the leaders of the new nation viewed Americans as a "chosen people," destined to demonstrate to the world how one nation could reflect the greater glory of God by creating a just and lasting society here in the New World.

A Great Seal was recommended for adoption on August 10, 1776, but formal acceptance did not take place until June 20, 1782. During this period, other committees viewed other designs and proposals. Today, the Great Seal of the United States consists of a bald eagle with raised wings, clutching in one talon a bundle of thirteen arrows and in the other an olive branch. Symbolically, the Great Seal suggests the power of the nation to declare war or make peace. Near the eagle's beak is the motto *E Pluribus Unum*. This motto was well-known in colonial America, having been used by *Gentlemen's Magazine*, a popular journal of the day.

The design for the reverse side of the Great Seal

The Great Seal of the United States features the national coat of arms (the American bald eagle with spread wings, holding an olive branch and arrows in its talons) and the Latin phrase E Pluribus Unum ("From Many, One").

was never cut, but what was proposed may be seen on the reverse side of the United States' one dollar bill. The design is of interest because it too shows how those who settled in the New World viewed their task. There is an encircled, unfinished pyramid above which is an eye surrounded by a halo of light. Below the pyramid are found the Latin phrases *Annuit Coeptis* (He has favored [our] undertaking) and *Novus Orde Seclorum* (A new order of the ages). These were not idle words. They demonstrate how men and women, the patriots of the new nation, were moved to reach far into the past for their inspiration and how they looked far into the future to identify a national destiny, one that would show the world the way to liberty and justice for all. The unfinished pyramid represents that America's task to live up to the promise of the American Creed is never finished, and the eye suggests that the conscience of America will be troubled until it does so.

The Bald Eagle

The bald eagle, so prominent on the Great Seal of the United States, was chosen by Congress to replace the British lion as the symbol of the nation as a whole. Adorned with arrows and olive branches, the bald eagle, it was thought, would encourage patriotic pride and symbolize "such needed values as superior courage, power, and authority. The eagle defied storms and commanded the air and had no equal in keenness of vision and in strength."[8]

The American bald eagle as a national symbol did not please everyone. Benjamin Franklin, for example, insisted that the eagle was a poor representative of what he hoped the United States would become. He said, "I wish the bald Eagle had not been chosen as the Representative of our Country; he is a Bird of bad moral character; like those among Men who live by sharping and Robbing, he is generally poor, and often very lousy. The Turkey is a more respectable Bird, and withall a true original Native of America."[9]

Nevertheless, before long the bald eagle caught the

patriotic imagination of Americans. Those who from time to time sought to omit, tamper with, or alter the bald eagle as a national symbol had to retreat under a barrage of patriotic fervor and protest. Franklin's objections notwithstanding, the eagle became clearly identified with the nation in cartoons and on balloons, coins, and paper currency.

THE FLAG

The American flag, now consisting of 50 white, five-pointed stars in a field of blue (representing each state of the nation) and thirteen alternating red and white stripes (representing each of the original states) is the paramount and most visible symbol of the nation. More than any other, it has borne the responsibility of fostering patriotism and of generating national unity and loyalty. Yet the flag that we recognize today is a product of gradual evolution. "No one can say with certainty who first proposed the familiar design, or when and where the Stars and Stripes were first unfurled."[10] The story of the role of Betsy Ross in designing the American flag at the request of George Washington cannot be proven to have actually taken place. It is an enduring patriotic myth that appears to have little basis in fact.

At first, the American flag had to compete with the flag of England, the flags of the American colonies, the flags of local militias, and the flags of congressional naval and land forces. When the first American ambassadors went to their posts abroad, they could not describe the American flag with any degree of clarity. "So much love, patriotism and sacrifice are symbolized in the flag that it is hard for present-day Americans to realize that it did not have some dramatic moment of birth."[11]

On New Year's Day, 1776, in a camp outside Boston, George Washington as commander in chief of the American forces first unfurled the Grand Union flag. This flag combined the elements of both British and American flags, thereby demonstrating that during the early days of the Revolution there remained a reluctance to give up the familiar symbolism associated with England. The Grand Union flag consisted of thirteen alternating red and white stripes, which represented the colonies, while in the corner were the traditional overlapped crosses of St. Andrew and St. George, which symbolized continued loyalty to the Crown. Actually, the Grand Union flag never flew over any major battlefield nor was it acceptable to Congress. Instead, on June 14, 1777, in Philadelphia, the Second Continental Congress adopted the following resolution: "The flag of the United States be made of thirteen stripes, alternate red and white; the union be 13 stars in a field of blue, representing a new constellation."

These 29 words were all that Congress at the time chose to say about the American flag. Nothing was said about size, nor how the flag should change, if at all, when new states were added to the Union. In 1793, Congress decided to add two new stripes and two new stars on the occasion of the admission of Vermont and Kentucky into the Union. For 25 years the flag of 15 stripes and 15 stars was the banner of the United States of America. In 1817, when it became evident that the flag could not continue to add new stripes, Congress reverted to the original flag by calling for thirteen alternating red and white stripes to represent the original states, while changing the field of blue by adding a star as new states were admitted. The "Stars and Stripes" during those years had been the flag only of the tiny United States Navy, and it was not until 1814 that the army adopted it as its banner as

The Grand Union Flag, also known as the Continental Colors, was America's first national flag (1775–77). It featured the British Union Jack in the upper left corner.

well. Not until the Mexican War (1846–48) did American soldiers fight under this single unifying emblem.

In 1812, Francis Scott Key wrote the "Star-Spangled Banner," a song that would not become the nation's anthem until over a century later. At the time it was written, however, it did much to encourage a growing reverence for the flag. Joseph Rodman Drake's poem "The American Flag," which first appeared in the *New York Evening Post* in 1819, provided early impetus for a growing sentiment to clothe

the flag in reverential homage. Others who contributed to the development of devotion to the American flag through their patriotic writings were such prominent American men and women of letters as Oliver Wendell Holmes, Julia Ward Howe, and John Greenleaf Whittier. Julia Ward Howe helped create the mood in which the flag came to be an emblem to be respected and revered when she wrote:

> *The flag of our stately battles, not struggles of wrath and greed.*
> *Its stripes were a holy lesson, its spangles a deathless creed.*
> *It is red with the blood of freemen and white with the fear of the foe,*
> *And the stars that fight in their courses 'gainst tyrants its symbols know.*

The military in uniform were expected to salute, civilian men to remove their hats, and all to place their right hands over their hearts when standing at attention to recite the Pledge of Allegiance. The flag came to symbolize bravery, courage, unity, freedom, liberty, hope, home, and, perhaps above all, America's destiny as a force for good in an otherwise evil world.

The Pledge of Allegiance

The Pledge of Allegiance to the flag was published initially in *Youth's Companion* on September 8, 1892. It appeared as part of a program, the National Public Schools Celebration of Columbus Day, which marked the four hundreth anniversary of the landing of Columbus in the New World. Francis Bellamy and James Upham, both staff members of *Youth's Companion*, claimed credit for the pledge. A dispute over

CASE STUDY:
BURNING THE AMERICAN FLAG

A code of etiquette on how the American flag should be displayed and the respect it was due, was not formally adopted by Congress until July 7, 1976. Despite these regulations, however, the Stars and Stripes has been displayed in commercial advertising contrary to the prescribed usage. Everything from T-shirts to bathing trunks to undershorts have been made to resemble the American flag. Major controversy about the use of the flag erupted in 1984 at the Republican National Convention in Dallas, Texas. In a demonstration Gregory Lee Johnson and a few others set fire to an American flag while intoning, "Red, white, and blue, we spit on you." Was this freedom of expression or were the demonstrators committing a punishable offense?

The demonstrators were charged with violating a Texas law forbidding the desecration of the flag. The U.S. Supreme Court in *Texas v. Johnson* (1989) by a 5–4 decision held that the act of burning the American flag was a form of freedom of expression and, as such, was protected by the First Amendment. The Texas law against violating the American flag was declared unconstitutional. Similar laws in 48 states were thus likewise held unconstitutional.

In 1989, in response to the Supreme Court decision, Congress passed the Flag Protection Act. At about the same time, the U.S. Senate tried, but failed, to begin the process of adding an amendment to the Constitution that would prohibit desecrating the flag. President George Bush, who had defeated his Democratic opponent, Michael Dukakis, partly on the basis of appearing more patriotic, favored a strongly worded amendment to prohibit flag burning. However, as the amendment attempt failed, he signed the Flag Protection Act because it was the best he could get. The act was immediately challenged by Sara Eichman, a political activist, and in the case of *United States v. Eichman* (1990) the U.S. Supreme Court declared the Flag Protection Act unconstitutional by a 5–4 vote.

Interest in the issue has since waned, and no amendment against desecrating the American flag is now under consideration. But the issue is dormant, not dead. Should an amendment against desecrating the flag be adopted?

Those who are against such an amendment believe that the flag itself represents the freedoms and values Americans cherish—above all freedom of expression—and, therefore, should not be held an exception to the First Amendment. Those who hold this view believe that if the flag is exempt from the First Amendment we may then be on a "slippery slope" that may, in other circumstances, exempt other actions from the protections of the Bill of Rights (the first ten amendments to the Constitution.) Those who favor such an amendment, including Steve Robertson, deputy director of the American Legion's Legislative Division, believe: "When you burn a flag, when you desecrate a synagogue or burn a cross, all you express is hatred. Nothing good comes out of burning."[12]

Professor Alan Brinkley of Columbia University has noted: "Battles over the flag have almost always been battles over how to define patriotism, and by implication, how to define America."[13] Brinkley goes on to declare: "Democracies secure in their identities and confident of their principles—as the United States was through much of its history— do not usually feel the need to define patriotism by law. But given the conspicuous absence of either security or confidence in contemporary American culture, no one should assume that the flag issue has been put to rest for good."[14] The decisions of the U.S. Supreme Court provide further evidence that in the United States patriotism cannot be coerced. Instead, patriotic sentiment and expression is a voluntary act of the individual.

---

who really wrote it continued for more than 40 years until a committee consisting of two historians and one political scientist studied the evidence and in 1939 concluded that Bellamy was properly the author. This finding was accepted by the American Flag Committee. The Pledge of Allegiance that Bellamy wrote was as follows: "I pledge allegiance to my Flag and to the Republic for which it stands, one nation, indivisible, with liberty and justice for all."

This original wording has been changed somewhat over the years. Some objected to the use of the word "my" because they felt that those who recited the pledge might not be swearing fealty to the flag of the United States of America. Instead, they might in secret be swearing loyalty to the flag of some foreign nation. This concern was of special importance to those who were uneasy about the many new immigrants who kept coming from southern and eastern Europe. The suspicion that these immigrants, who spoke a strange language and who seemed slow in learning English, might have harbored continuing loyalty to a hostile power was, in the main, a reflection of the rising anti-immigrant sentiment of the time. Nevertheless, in response to these fears, the pledge was changed; "my" was replaced by "the Flag of the United States of America." Another change was made by House Joint Resolution 243, which required that the words "under God" be inserted after "one Nation." This was accomplished on June 14, 1954, when President Dwight Eisenhower approved the resolution.

In its present form, the Pledge of Allegiance harks back to the Republic, the Declaration of Independence, and the Constitution of the United States. The pledge is made "to the Flag of the United States of America" and not to any particular individual or any political group that happens to be in power at the time. The pledge is made to a republican form of government, that is, a government without a king, and to an indivisible nation whose unity was tested in a bloody civil war. The words "under God" remind us of the deep religious sentiments that guided the development of the nation when a "New Jerusalem" and a "New Israel" were to be established in the New World. And, most importantly, once again there is a pledge to work toward liberty and justice, not just for all Americans, but for all people everywhere. The latter reaffirms the mission and continuing destiny of the American nation.

Just as the U.S. Supreme Court held that laws protecting the flag from desecration were unconstitutional inasmuch as they were violations of freedom of expression, so the same court held that the pledge could not be required by those whose religion or conscience called upon them to refrain from doing so.

The National Anthem

"If I may write the ballads of a people," said Andrew Fletcher of Scotland, "I care not who writes its laws." Although this may be something of an overstatement, it is in the songs of a nation that the honor and glory and spirit and courage of a nation are often enshrined and passed on from generation to generation. Let us see how this applies to "The Star-Spangled Banner," our national anthem.

Perhaps no inspirational message contributed more to the growth of American patriotism than did the song written by Francis Scott Key during the early days of the War of 1812. The star-spangled banner that Key glorified was one of fifteen stripes and fifteen stars. It was 30 by 42 feet, made of 400 yards of hand-woven wool bunting and sewn expressly for Fort McHenry by Mary Young Pickersgill of Baltimore,

Maryland. But the song about this banner only gradually won the affection of the American people and remains somewhat controversial to this day.

Francis Scott Key was an attorney and the son-in-law of Chief Justice Roger Taney of the U.S. Supreme Court. He sought and received permission from President James Madison to board the British flagship then anchored in Baltimore harbor where, under a truce agreement, he would try to secure the release of Dr. William Beanes, who was being held a prisoner on board for allegedly insulting British officers. Key was allowed to board the ship in the company of Colonel John S. Skinner, who had arranged for his safe conduct. Key and Skinner managed to secure the release of Beanes, but the party was denied permission to return immediately to Baltimore. The British feared that during the course of their activities on the ship, these men had heard of a forthcoming attack on Fort McHenry and would warn the occupants of the fort. Beanes, Skinner, and Key were detained in the skiff they had used to go out to the British man-of-war.

While seated in the tiny boat, the men had a clear view of "the rockets' red glare" and of "the bombs bursting in air," whose brilliance gave proof "through the night" that "the flag was still there." When the bombardment ended, after almost 25 hours during which some 1,500 shells—some of which weighed 220 pounds—were exploded, the men were relieved to see "by the dawn's early light" that the "broad stripes and bright stars" of the flag still waved above Fort McHenry.

The War of 1812 triggered a good deal of patriotic emotion among the American people. The new nation was asserting itself against humiliations to which the British had subjected it, such as the defeat of the USS *Chesapeake* by the British ship *Leopard* in 1807, when the British boarded the *Chesapeake* and

What so proudly we hail'd at the twilight's last gleaming,
hose broad stripes & bright stars through the perilous fight
'er the ramparts we watch'd, were so gallantly streamin
And the rocket's red glare, the bomb bursting in ai
Gave proof through the night that our flag was still ther
O say does that star spangled banner yet wave
O'er the land of the free & the home of the brave?

On the shore dimly seen through the mists of the de
Where the foe's haughty host in dread silence repo
What is that which the breeze, o'er the towering steep,
As it fitfully blows, half conceals half discloses?
Now it catches the gleam of the morning's first bea
In full glory reflected now shines in the stream
'Tis the star-spangled banner — O long may it wav
O'er the land of the free & the home of the brave

And where is that band who so vauntingly swore,
That the havoc of war & the battle's confusion
A home & a Country should leave us no more?
Their blood has wash'd out their foul footsteps po
No refuge could save the hireling & slave
From the terror of flight or the gloom of the grav
And the star-spangled banner in triumph doth wave
O'er the land of the free & the home of the brav

O thus be it ever when freemen shall stand
Between their lov'd home & the war's desolation!
Blest with vict'ry & peace may the heav'n rescued la
Praise the power that hath made & preserv'd us a na
Then conquer we must when our cause it is jus
And this be our motto — "In God is our trust,"
And the star-spangled banner in triumph shall wave

This is the original draft of the "Star-Spangled Banner" in Francis Scott Key's handwriting. The "Star-Spangled Banner" did not become the national anthem until 1931.

removed four Americans they said were deserters. This humiliation was avenged when Captain James Lawrence aboard the same *Chesapeake* defeated the British ship *Shannon* in 1812. Lawrence was killed in the fray but his words, "Don't give up the ship," encouraged Commander Oliver Hazard Perry to make a flag of Lawrence's dying words and use it to rally his fleet to defeat the British on Lake Erie. And the USS *Constitution*, the most famous American ship of all, defeated the *Guerriere*, the *Java*, the *Wasp*, and the *Frolic*. While these naval victories did little to alter the course or outcome of the war, they did arouse much patriotic fervor among Americans.

In this emotionally charged environment, Francis Scott Key jotted down words and phrases that described Fort McHenry under bombardment, and when safely in his hotel room, he completed the words and adapted the music of "Anacreon in Heaven," a well-known drinking song of the day written by an Englishman named John Stafford Smith. Originally, the song was called "The Defense of Fort McHenry," but the following January 6, just before the Battle of New Orleans, it was given its current title, "The Star-Spangled Banner." The song was sung publicly for the first time on October 19, 1814.

Despite its early popularity, it competed for many years for acceptance with such patriotic songs as "America," "Hail Columbia," "Yankee Doodle," and "Marching through Georgia." When on January 30, 1913, Jefferson Levy introduced a bill in Congress to make "The Star-Spangled Banner" our national anthem, the proposal died in committee. In 1916, President Wilson gave the song some official recognition when he chose it for state occasions. Thus, during World War I, while it was not yet our national anthem, it did have a special place. Between 1910 and

1930, thirty-five bills were introduced to make "The Star-Spangled Banner" our national anthem. The objections over the years were many. Only on March 3, 1931, did Congress pass a bill that officially recognized "The Star-Spangled Banner" as the anthem of the nation. When adopted, America was in the throes of a depression and little note was taken by the people as a whole. Not until World War II prompted an outburst of patriotic sentiment did the national anthem become widely known and more frequently performed.

Most people mistakenly believe that "The Star-Spangled Banner" was the national anthem from the time it was written. Because of its relatively recent adoption as the nation's anthem, from time to time proposals are made to replace it. In 1984 Representative Andrew Jacobs Jr. of Indiana filed a bill to replace it, but his proposal was not adopted.

What are some of the objections to "The Star-Spangled Banner?" Some object to the fact that the music was written by an Englishman and not by an American. Those knowledgeable about music say that it is a very difficult tune for many people to sing, so difficult that on occasion it has even been troublesome for opera singers. Others insist that the poem on which the anthem is based is of low quality, that it represents a single, not so very important incident in American history, and that it is warlike in character. For example, do we want to trigger the American collective patriotic memory with bursting rockets and bombs? In addition, words to the song in the third stanza—which include: "Their blood has wash'd out their footsteps pollution / No refuge could save the hireling and slave / From the terror of flight or the gloom of the grave"—appear particularly offensive. Is it not almost racist to suggest that the British have "polluted" these shores? And, is this a fair way to comment about a nation with whom America has had a long-standing "special relationship?"

Among suggested alternatives to "The Star-Spangled Banner" is "America the Beautiful," the lyrics of which were written by Katharine Lee Bates and the music by Samuel Augustus Ward, both Americans. The music is simpler to sing, the thoughts peaceful in nature and more in keeping with the essential American character.[15]

In the fourth stanza of "The Star-Spangled Banner" are the lines: "Then conquer we must, when our cause it is just, / And this be our motto: 'In God is our trust.' " During the Civil War, Secretary of the Treasury Salmon P. Chase adapted the expression "In God We Trust," when he authorized its use on American coins as a morale building measure as Union forces were suffering military defeats. The motto first appeared on some coins in 1864, but it was not until 1955 that Congress authorized its use on all coins and paper currency. In 1956, "In God We Trust" became the national motto of the United States. The use of the motto has not been without controversy because to some it appears to be a violation of the First Amendment which reads, "Congress shall make no law respecting an establishment of religion or prohibiting the free exercise thereof."

Our national symbols also have taken shape in our country's monuments. Because these often become civic shrines to which many Americans make frequent pilgrimages as a means of recalling their national history; transmitting the national heritage to their children and grandchildren; recognizing heroes, heroines, and pivotal turning points in the nation's history; and expressing their patriotism, let us see how America has sought to remember in more concrete form.

FIVE

NATIONAL MONUMENTS AND AMERICAN PATRIOTISM

[W]e are assembled to protest against a form of government existing without the consent of the governed—to declare our right to be free as man is free, to be represented in the government which we are taxed to support, to have such disgraceful laws as give man the power to chastise and imprison his wife, to take the wages which she earns, the property which she inherits, and in case of separation, the children of her love; laws which make her the mere dependent on his bounty. It is to protest against such unjust laws as these that we are assembled today, and to have them, if possible, forever erased.

— Elizabeth Cady Stanton, keynote address to the Women's Rights Convention, Seneca Falls, New York (1848)

According to its Latin roots, the term "monument" means "things that remind." Unlike some countries, the United States has erected comparatively few national monuments to serve as symbolic reminders of glorious moments in history. Cities and states do have statues and other concrete memorials to prominent heroes and heroines, war veterans, and others who have made memorable contributions in community service.

But at the national level, funds for monuments have been limited. Most have been built only after seemingly interminable debate, and then only through the persistence of a zealous few who determined that a particular individual or event should be fixed in memory with an appropriate monument. According to Merle Curti, "[n]ational monuments never became so enshrined in the American heart, never symbolized in the same way loyalty to the nation,"[1] as did the symbolism of the flag or anthem.

The building of national monuments has been left mainly to the fund-raising efforts of private citizens. The government has intervened to make construction possible by using the power of law to clear land and provide zoning variances. Private corporations have contributed millions of dollars toward the construction of monuments, but Americans have sometimes seen corporate money as being somehow tainted. Some people question whether a giant corporation that donates funds to build a monument should have certain privileges in using the monument in advertising or in otherwise profiting from its generosity? Although we rely largely on the private sector to build our national monuments, there is always tension as ordinary Americans sometimes feel that corporate America has "bought" their national shrines.

But the funds of corporate America alone have rarely been adequate to the task of building monuments, so mass appeals have been made and often even schoolchildren have been asked to give their coins. As a result of this ambivalence about who should pay for monuments, how much they should cost, and who will maintain them, some monuments took decades, even generations, to complete.

Because there is little agreement about the role monuments should play in a republic, nearly all national monuments were marked with controversy as to the appropriateness of their design, size, artistic merit or lack thereof, location, and purpose. Jared Clark Markham, who designed the Saratoga Battlefield monument along the upper Hudson River, had this to say about the role of monuments in the United States:

> *Monuments erected by the Republic should have a broader character and far deeper interest than those of monarchy. Being truly the work of the people, they should record the traditions of the people as to build up a true national art, a high tone and spirit, a pride of nationality, a pure and lofty patriotism. Hence it will be seen that we have no precedents to guide us in our monuments; that like our Constitution and our laws, they must grow out of the character and requirements of the people.*[2]

The designs of monuments have been diverse, but it should come as no surprise that just as the nation's founders drew on Greece and Rome for their inspiration when designing the national seal, so too, these ancient nations were drawn on as models for monument building in the nation's capital and elsewhere. Visitors to Washington, D.C., can see that its buildings and monuments remain largely Greek and Roman in character, while portraits and statues of national heroes often depict them wearing the Roman toga and laurel wreath.

The Liberty Bell is something of an exception to these principles. But because it became a monument to American independence at the very founding of the nation, our review of some of the major national monuments will begin with a closer look at how the Liberty Bell was transformed into an important national symbol.

THE LIBERTY BELL

Bells have long been used for symbolic and ceremonial occasions in many countries, but few bells anywhere have enjoyed the reverential homage that has been paid to the Liberty Bell. Located in Independence Hall in Philadelphia, where the Declaration of Independence was signed and proclaimed, the Liberty Bell, as it came to be called, only gradually laid claim to the patriotic emotions of the American people.

In Philadelphia, it was the custom to summon the people and members of the colonial assembly together by means of a bell. When the city commemorated the fiftieth anniversary of the 1701 charter that Pennsylvania received from the British Crown, a grand bell was sought to mark the occasion. At the same time, funds were appropriated to build a new state house, where the bell would be kept and where the seat of colonial government would reside. The bell, weighing about a ton, was cast in England and shipped to Philadelphia, where it arrived in August 1752. During the early trials, the bell cracked and needed to be recast. The recasting was done in America, and more copper was added to make the bell less brittle. Inscribed on the bell is, "Proclaim Liberty throughout all the land and unto all the inhabitants thereof."

This statement from the Bible (Leviticus 25:10) was meant to rally further support for the liberties the charter provided to the people of Pennsylvania. That its inscription later fit so well with the meaning and spirit of the Declaration of Independence was entirely coincidental.

The one-ton bell, not really very big or loud compared with some of the world's great bells, was in frequent use in Pennsylvania, so much so that colonists who lived nearby often complained about the noise. Yet, as the American Revolution approached, the bell called the men and women of Philadelphia together to tell them about what was taking place throughout the colonies in the growing dispute with Britain.

On February 3, 1757, the bell rang when Benjamin Franklin left for England to see if there was any flexibility in the position or attitude of Great Britain toward her American colonies. On October 5, 1765, it rang again, calling upon the colonists to resist the stamp tax. The bell rang on February 4, 1771, to emphasize the opposition of Philadelphia to the tax on tea. And again on December 27, 1773, it rang when the ship *Poly* with its "odious cargo" of tea sailed into Philadelphia harbor. The people of that city refused to unload the tea, and the captain had to take the vessel elsewhere. On June 1, 1774, the bell rang when the people of Philadelphia agreed to send help to the city of Boston, then under siege by British troops. It rang again on April 25, 1775, when the people of Philadelphia heard about the Battle of Lexington.

The Declaration of Independence was adopted on July 4, 1776, but the bell was not rung because no public announcement was made. It took time to assemble all the signatures and to have the document printed for widespread distribution. Without radio, the news that independence had been declared was not instantaneously communicated to the American people. Although July 4 is observed as American Independence Day, it was only on July 8 that the first public reading of the Declaration was made to the sounds of the tolling of the great bell.

During the war, when British general William

Howe was about to occupy Philadelphia, safekeeping was sought for the bell. In a train of seven hundred wagons the entire Second Continental Congress moved out of Philadelphia and took the bell with them. The bell was hidden in a church in Allentown, Pennsylvania, for a year before it was returned to Philadelphia after the British had left. On October 24, 1781, the bell rang again to celebrate the defeat of the British general Lord Cornwallis at Yorktown.

The bell continued to be rung at critical turning points in American history. It rang on November 27, 1781, when General George Washington and his wife, Martha, arrived in Philadelphia after the long trip from Virginia. It was rung again on September 3, 1783, announcing the peace treaty between America and Britain. It rang on July 4, 1788, to celebrate the adoption of the Constitution and again on December 18, 1799, when George Washington died. It rang on February 19, 1801, when Thomas Jefferson was elected President and again in 1804 news reached Philadelphia that Alexander Hamilton had been killed in his duel with Aaron Burr. It rang on September 29, 1824, when the Marquis de Lafayette, the French general who supported the Revolution and helped George Washington, visited the city. It rang again on July 4, 1826 marking the fiftieth anniversary of the Declaration of Independence.

By this time the bell showed signs of metal fatigue, but it rang on Independence Day, 1831, and again on February 22, 1832, to mark the birthday of George Washington. It rang in 1832 when Charles Carroll, the last signer of the Declaration of Independence, died, and it tolled the funeral notes on July 2, 1834, when Lafayette died. It rang on July 8, 1835, the fifty-ninth anniversary of the first public reading of the Declaration of Independence as well as in

The Liberty Bell cracked in 1835. It remains the symbol of American patriotism

solemn recognition of the death of U.S. Supreme Court chief justice John Marshall. When it was rung on this occasion, the bell cracked. It had rung for the last time.

Today, the Liberty Bell, so named in 1852, rings no more. It may be struck with a wooden or rubber mallet to evoke a rather melodious note, but it can no longer be truly rung. If the heart of the nation is symbolized in its flag, and the soul of the nation in its anthem, then the voice of the nation may be symbolized in its bells. Among these the Liberty Bell has won a preeminent place in the hearts of American patriots.

The Bunker Hill Monument

When a monument was proposed to commemorate the Battle of Bunker Hill (June 17, 1775), an early battle of the Revolution fought on the outskirts of Boston, there was much debate about what the monument should look like and long delay before it was built. The Bunker Hill Monument may be the first in which a group of prominent people sought in a conscious way to jostle the American memory and to encourage American patriotism.

In 1825, after a good deal of haggling about funds and solicitation of funds from the public, enough money was raised to make it possible to lay the cornerstone of the monument. Daniel Webster, one of the leading orators of his day, gave one of his great speeches. On that occasion Webster said, "Let our object be our country; our whole country, and nothing but our country. And, by the blessing of God, may that country itself become a vast and splendid monument, not of oppression and terror, but of wisdom, of peace, and of liberty upon which the world may gaze with admiration forever." Some two hundred veterans of the American Revolution and forty participants in the Battle of Bunker Hill marched in a grand parade. The cheers of those who lined the parade route brought tears to the eyes of the marchers.

Yet enthusiasm soon abated and the flow of money slowed to a trickle. The monument was not completed until 1843. Only the efforts and sustained interest of a small group of people saw to the completion of the monument. Among the interesting aspects of the fund-raising process was the participation of women in and around Boston. This was one of the earliest examples in America of women organizing themselves and sponsoring a gigantic fair on behalf of a monument. At least one writer believes that the women, "humbly patriotic . . . put over the project."[3] Fund-raising efforts by women were an early aspect of the modern feminist movement, which led to the Seneca Falls convention.

President John Tyler and his cabinet attended the dedication of the Bunker Hill Monument, and the president marched in a long parade of war veterans, other military units, and a large number of fraternal and educational organizations. About 100,000 people heard Daniel Webster once again express his view that the Bunker Hill Monument stood for "patriotism and courage," and for "civil and religious liberty." "Thank God," he said, "I, I also am an American."[4]

The Bunker Hill Monument is essentially a statue of Colonel William Prescott, who led the American troops in the Battle of Bunker Hill. Prescott and his band of colonial soldiers held the British troops under General Howe at bay as the British made two successive charges up the hill. On the third charge, with their ammunition almost gone, Prescott and his men were overwhelmed and retreated to a nearby hill. Although the Battle of Bunker Hill was a defeat in which about 450 Americans were killed or wounded, it did demonstrate what determined colonials could do. Little wonder then at the pride the American colonists took in that early battle of the Revolution.

Inscribed on the monument is: "This hand opposed to tyrants searches with a sword for peaceful conditions under liberty." Today, the memory of the Battle of Bunker Hill still resonates despite the urban growth around the monument site, which makes it difficult to recall the spirit the monument seeks to evoke, the memory of those who died, and the purpose for which they fought.

WASHINGTON MONUMENT

When the Revolution ended there were those in the Continental Congress who wanted to honor General George Washington for his leadership during the war. They proposed that a statue be erected of Washington on horseback in Roman dress with a truncheon in one hand and a laurel wreath encircling his head. Washington opposed this design and urged that it be abandoned, citing more pressing use of the nation's limited funds. When, however, Pierre-Charles L'Enfant was appointed to draw up the plans for the nation's capital, a place was provided where a monument to George Washington could be erected.

Eight days after Washington's death, Representative John Marshall, who later became the second and perhaps most distinguished chief justice of the U.S. Supreme Court, proposed that "a marble monument be erected by the United States in the Capitol, that the family of George Washington be requested to permit the body to be deposited under it."[5] Nothing substantive came of the proposal.

For 30 years, however, the matter of how to honor Washington was debated, but no decision could be reached. In 1833, a group decided to take matters out of the hands of Congress, and they organized the Washington National Monument Society. Chief

Justice John Marshall and President James Madison served as presidents of this group for short periods of time. The society envisioned a monument costing about a million dollars, asked for designs to be submitted, and sought to raise money through private donations.

The society appointed collection agents for each state and territory. To be certain that the monument would reflect the popular will, contributions were limited, at first, to a $1 per year from any one person. By 1847, the sum of $87,000 had been raised and the society thought it had enough money at least to begin work on the monument.

Most of the designs were grandly flamboyant in accordance with the tastes and standards of the day. The successful design was submitted by Robert Mills, an early American architect, whose proposal consisted of a monument resembling an Egyptian obelisk atop of which would be a statue of Washington in a Roman chariot drawn by four horses. Around the obelisk would be thirty columns that would provide space for the addition of other national heroes.

In January 1848, 64 years after the initial proposal to build a monument in memory of George Washington, Congress granted the Washington National Monument Society a 37-acre site and authorized it to proceed with the project. In that year the cornerstone was laid amidst elaborate ceremonies in which President James K. Polk played a leading role. Because of lack of funds, construction stopped in 1854, and the onset of the Civil War postponed the project indefinitely. Because there was little money to continue, the monument was simplified, the rotunda was eliminated, and the obelisk was reduced by a hundred feet. For more than 20 years the Washington Monument remained unfinished.

The Washington Monument towers over the nation's capital. The monument was completed in 1884.

However, on July 5, 1876, in a spate of patriotism and an awareness that the centennial year of the nation's founding was at hand, Congress authorized that work be resumed and appropriated funds to make that possible. According to the resolution introduced by John Sherman:

> *As a mark of our sense of honor due his name and his compatriots and associates, our Revolutionary fathers, we, the Senate and House of Representatives, in Congress assembled, and in the name of the people of the United States, at this, the beginning of the second century of national existence, do assume and direct the completion of the Washington Monument in the city of Washington.*[6]

In place of the statue of Washington driving a chariot, a 3,000-pound pyramid of pure aluminum—the largest ever used at that time—was put at the capstone. On December 6, 1884, the Washington Monument was completed. Though Washington had been "First in war, first in peace, and first in the hearts of his countrymen," the process of building the monument honoring him had been painfully slow as money was grudgingly made available and as enthusiasm waxed and waned. Today, however, the Washington Monument is an important symbol not only to Americans but to people from all parts of the globe, who can be seen standing in long lines, most often with their children, for the privilege of climbing the stairs or taking the elevator to the very top. As they look out and survey the landscape of the American capital, the memory of the nation's accomplishments may be rekindled and the nation's heritage shared with the next generation.

The Statue of Liberty and Ellis Island

Dedicated by President Grover Cleveland on October 28, 1886, *Liberty Enlightening the World*, or the Statue of Liberty, was a gift from France to America. In part it was a gesture of French-American friendship, and in part an attempt by French political leaders to influence French public opinion toward reestablishing a French republic and away from monarchy.

Designed by Frédéric-Auguste Bartholdi, the Statue of Liberty, with its commanding position at the entrance to New York harbor on Liberty Island, was intended as a monument to the best in America. With its huge size (151 feet high, 225 tons), its outstretched arm holding aloft a torch, and its other arm holding a tablet that bears the date of the Declaration of Independence, the Statue of Liberty symbolizes the American Creed and the freedoms for which the nation stands. For American travelers, it is the moment their ship passes the Statue of Liberty that they finally say good-bye to their homeland, and it is the Statue of Liberty that greets them upon their safe return. For those few immigrants who still arrive by ship, it welcomes those seeking a better life in America. On its pedestal a poem by Emma Lazarus appears, part of which reads: "Give me your tired, your poor, / Your huddled masses yearning to breathe free."

In France, enthusiasm for the proposed Statue of Liberty was high, and the Union Franco-Americaine had raised the $400,000 needed to design and build the statue. In America, however, there was a good deal of foot-dragging, and it took some time before the American Committee was established to work with the Union Franco-Americaine. Made up of distinguished Americans, the committee was assigned the task of raising $125,000 to build the pedestal upon which the statue would stand. In February 1877, Congress approved the site for the statue and funds for its maintenance, but money for building the pedestal had to come from private sources. The family of John Jacob Astor, whose fortune was based on the fur trade; Cyrus W. Field, who laid the first transatlantic cable; Andrew Carnegie, who established United States Steel Corporation; and P. T. Barnum, who created the circus in America, were among the elite who led America's fund-raising effort. But the wealthy donors alone couldn't quite raise the money, because the cost of the pedestal kept increasing. Because Americans did not have a tradition of monument building—remember that the Washington Monument had barely been completed after a harrowing history of postponement—they remained apathetic and did not share the ardor for the project that was exhibited across the sea.

In France, by March 1885, the Statue of Liberty was packed and awaiting shipment, but in America the project was on the verge of collapsing until the timely intervention of Joseph Pulitzer, a Hungarian immigrant and the publisher of the *New York World* newspaper. Until Pulitzer lent his efforts to the fund-raising drive it had been largely a project of the rich and the famous. His idea was to appeal to the masses of Americans and to schoolchildren, and he used his newspaper to stimulate patriotic sentiment on behalf of the statue. "Gather in the money, dollar by dollar, dime by dime, penny by penny," he wrote in the *World*. "See what the children are doing. A nine-year-old boy collected $7 from his father's employees; a thirteen-year-old girl raised funds from among hundreds of her schoolmates; a grammar-school girl made her papa, her brother and all the family subscribe, as well as all the people who came into her papa's store."[7]

By August 11, 1885, Pulitzer gleefully announced that he had raised the required $100,000 and that more than 120,000 people had contributed. Thus, through Pulitzer's vision and fund-raising zeal, the Statue of Liberty became a project of the people. Indeed, so popular did the project become that the *New York World* was given a significant boost in circulation at a time when it was most needed.

Native Americans called it Gull Island, but it is known as Ellis Island, named for the man who owned the island in the late 18th century. New York State bought the island from Samuel Ellis and fortified it to defend its harbor. It later ceded the island to the federal government for $10,000.

Ellis Island is renowned as the place through which many immigrants passed en route to new lives in America. Opened in 1892 as an immigration processing center, the island could handle as many as 5,000 immigrants a day, and during one day in 1907, at the peak of immigration, 11,000 men, women, and children waited to learn whether they would be admitted to what Russian immigrant author Mary Antin called "the Promised Land." During the height of immigration to America, between 1892 and 1924, some 12 million immigrants passed through Ellis Island. About 40 percent of all Americans today are descendants of those immigrants, for whom Ellis Island meant hope for a new life in America.[8] After the United States essentially stopped immigration in 1924, little use was made of the island and it was officially closed in 1954. But how could a facility that meant so much to so many be abandoned?

In 1965, responsibility for Ellis Island and the Statue of Liberty National Monument was assigned to the National Park Service, and in 1976 visitors began touring the facilities. In 1982, President Ronald Reagan

Fireworks burst around the Statue of Liberty during Fourth of July celebrations in 1986.

asked Lee Iacocca, former chairman of the Chrysler Corporation, to seek private funds to restore the Statue of Liberty and Ellis Island, and in 1984, a $60 million dollar repair and restoration project began.

On September 10, 1990, Ellis Island was reopened amidst much fanfare, fireworks, and celebration. Today, visitors can walk where their forebears walked and can get the feeling of what it was like to be among the "masses yearning to breathe free." Little wonder that visitors to Ellis Island are shown an orientation film with the perceptive title "Island of Hope—Island of Tears," which sympathetically captures the hardships immigrants endured, the hurt of those who were turned away mostly because they were physically unfit, and the uplifted spirits of those who were allowed to enter America. Ellis Island is a national monument to the dramatic history of American immigration.

The renovation of the Statue of Liberty and Ellis Island was not without controversy. Although they are administered by the National Park Service, as are other national monuments, funds came mostly from private sources. Some members of Congress feared that the Statue of Liberty renovation and the re-creation of Ellis Island would involve a "corporate takeover of an American shrine." The controversy, however, was but an echo of that of more than a century ago when Pulitzer had to step in to rescue the Statue of Liberty.

In America, without government funding, for better or worse we rely on handsome gifts from private corporations, as well as on more broad support from individual Americans and from schoolchildren. Steven Briganti, vice president of the Statue of Liberty–Ellis Island Foundation, defends corporate support for the effort to restore and create these national monuments: "We are proud of our corporate sponsors. The

Statue of Liberty stands for everything America is . . . the capitalist system with appropriate use being made of commercialism."[9] Nearly every monument in America has been caught up in the tension between raising funds through corporate and other private sources and establishing a symbol in which all Americans might share.

Among the problems in generating enthusiasm and raising money for the Statue of Liberty was the fact that it was to rise in New York harbor. It was difficult to convince Americans that *Liberty Enlightening the World* was intended as a gift for all, not for the people of New York alone. While people from all over the United States come to visit it, the thought expressed in 1924 by Ralph Barton Perry is not without merit. It would be better, he said, if the Statue of Liberty were "removed to the interior, there to revolve upon its pedestal and to stir the aspirations of Americans. . . . Thus placed, it would symbolize not liberty attained . . . but that liberty which is our goal. It might then . . . symbolize our seeking and our confessing of shortcomings, our faith and our candor, and before, the world, our tolerance and comradeship."[10]

The Lincoln Memorial

Our sixteenth president, Abraham Lincoln, is best known for being president during the Civil War, for his Gettysburg Address, and for signing the Emancipation Proclamation, which freed the slaves in the states that had left the Union. It is something of a paradox that the dedication of his memorial should have been held during the 1920s, when race relations in America were at a nadir, segregation rampant, and racism rife. The Lincoln Memorial is unusual in the United States, in that substantial funds for building the Lincoln Memorial came from government. Nevertheless, it was more than 50 years after Lincoln's death that a memorial to his memory was finally dedicated.

The story of the building of the Lincoln Memorial begins two years after Lincoln's death. On March 29, 1867, Congress incorporated the Lincoln Monument Association and charged it with the responsibility of erecting a monument in the nation's capital "commemorative of the great charter of emancipation and universal liberty in America."[11] However, little was accomplished except some modest fund-raising and some study of monuments in America and abroad. Progress was slow until February 9, 1911, when the president signed a bill creating a Lincoln Memorial Commission "to procure and determine upon a location, plan, and design for a monument or memorial . . . to the memory of Abraham Lincoln."[12]

President William Howard Taft was chosen chairman of the commission and the sum of $50,000 was immediately made available. In due course, Congress appropriated $300,000, and ground for the Lincoln Memorial was broken at noon on Lincoln's birthday (February 12) in 1914. Henry Bacon designed the memorial, and the sculptor Daniel Chester French created the heroic statue of Lincoln. On Memorial Day, May 30, 1922, the Lincoln Memorial was dedicated. Through the startling new medium of radio, thousands of Americans could participate in the dedication ceremony. They heard Dr. Robert R. Moton, principal of Tuskegee Institute, speak of issues that are as timely today as they were when he spoke to the assembled throng. Moton drew on Lincoln's second inaugural address for inspiration: "With malice toward none, with charity for all, with firmness in the right as God give us to see the right," he declared, "I somehow believe that all of us, black and white, both North and South, are

Daniel Chester French's statue of Abraham Lincoln is located inside the Lincoln Memorial.

going to strive on to finish the work which he so nobly began, to make America an example for the world of equal opportunity for all who strive and are willing to serve under the flag that makes men free."[13]

Case Study:
The Vietnam Memorial Monument

The Vietnam War (1964–73) was the most controversial war in U.S. history and the nation's only military defeat. It is not surprising that the memorial to it should likewise be surrounded with controversy and marked by the passion and emotion that characterized the war itself.

Does an unpopular war deserve a national monument? What is an appropriate way, if any, to memorialize a national defeat? How should tribute be paid to the 541,000 who were drafted or volunteered for military service to the nation? What is the best way to honor the young Americans who died and the many more who were wounded? And were the deaths wasted in a futile or unnecessary war, or did those who died make a sacrifice in defense of their country? In short, what should the nation remember about the Vietnam War?

In 1979, Jan Scruggs, a private; Tom Carhart, a West Point graduate; and other Vietnam veterans living in the Washington, D.C., area conceived the idea that a memorial should be built to those who died or were wounded in that unpopular struggle. In attempting to achieve their goal, they did not initially grasp how formidable an effort they would have to make.

A Vietnam Veterans Memorial Foundation was established to identify a site and begin the tedious process of raising money. There were many in official Washington who thought that building a monument was a good idea and so it seemed that such a monument could be built speedily and without much conflict. But this was clearly not the case. Some saw the monument as a chance of massaging the patriotic nerve of America. Others saw it as a means of national reconciliation to heal the emotional wounds and divisiveness that the war had created. Others saw it as a memorial to the valor, heroism, and self-sacrifice of those who had served in the military. Still others saw it as a memorial to those who died. But some thought it should stand as evidence of America's breach of faith with the people and as a reminder that those who opposed the war and refused to serve had also been performing a patriotic duty.

Ross Perot, a wealthy businessman and twice a presidential candidate, paid for the competition in which the design was selected. A jury to judge the proposals was selected, but no Vietnam veteran was included. According to the rules of the competition, designers were told: "The memorial will make no political statement regarding the war or its conduct. It will transcend those issues. The hope is that the creation of the memorial will begin a healing process, a reconciliation of the grievous divisions wrought by the war."[14] A young woman from Yale, Maya Ying Lin, won the award for her design of two long, black granite walls that intersect to form a V. One wall points to the Washington Monument, a symbol of independence, the other to the Lincoln Memorial, a symbol of reconciliation. On these walls are inscribed the names of each of the fifty-eight thousand men and women who died in Southeast Asia between 1957 and 1975. The names are listed chronologically in the order in which they died.

No sooner had the design been accepted than a torrent of conflict ensued. Ross Perot was critical that the design paid tribute only to the "guys that died" and not to the heroism of those who took part. He withdrew from the project. James Webb, a secretary of the navy and longtime supporter of the war, described it as a "mass grave." Carhart himself, his West Point background showing, called it a "black gash of shame." Eventually, a compromise was worked out: a flag was added, a heroic statue of three soldiers from the Vietnam War was built, and the inscription "God Bless America" was inscribed on the monument itself.

On November 7, 1982, veterans and others began to filter into Washington, D.C., in anticipation of the dedication ceremony, which was held on November 13. Compared with other parades held at dedication ceremonies, the march was distinct-

A small flag and a rose serve as a rememberance of slain soldiers.

ly disorderly as some protested the war while others protested the monument. The parade's theme, "Marching Along Together," was scarcely in evidence.

Built at a cost of about $7 million dollars, which were raised privately, the monument stands in the Washington Mall. In a city of monuments it has, in a short period of time, won the tribute of visitors. Those who feel deeply about the war or those who lost someone near and dear to them come to the wall to remember, to think. Some leave letters; others leave pictures, a teddy bear, or cowboy boots.

To this day the debate continues over a war that lives in memory as a painful episode in the nation's history. The Vietnam Memorial teeters on the razor's edge between being a shrine to which those who come "to find peace with [myself] and spend some time with my memories,"[15] and those who are inspired by it as a further expression of American patriotism.

The Jefferson Memorial in Washington, D.C., the Tomb of the Unknown Soldier in Alexandria, Virginia, the faces of Washington, Jefferson, Lincoln, and Theodore Roosevelt at Mount Rushmore in South Dakota, all serve to encourage patriotic expression among Americans. It is in the spirit of American patriotism that American monuments mean different things to different people at different times. They are magnets for those who use them as rallying points to call upon the nation to meet current challenges and solve current problems. It was at the Washington Monument on August 28, 1963, to a crowd of about 250,000 people that the Reverend Martin Luther King Jr. declared: "I have a dream that one day this nation will rise up and live out the true meaning of its creed—we hold these truths to be self-evident that all men are created equal."

Six

Our Ceremonial Calendar

Patriotism in America seems to be "old hat." If a man gets out and waves the American flag, he is now "suspect" or called a "reactionary." We applaud the nationalistic demonstrations in other countries. Perhaps we need a few demonstrations for America.

—Evangelist Billy Graham

On patriotic holidays, Americans often use the time to take a swim, play some golf or tennis, go shopping, paint the house, or mow the lawn. Yet the patriotic holidays resonate in the hearts of ordinary men and women and keep the flame of patriotism burning, sometimes brightly, sometimes dimly, but never entirely disappearing.

During the 17th century nearly all the holidays observed in the American colonies were religious. Many were fast days, some were feast days, but in either case they represented expressions of sacrifice or thanks to God for having saved the colonies from natural calamities, such as poor harvests, violent weather, epidemics of illness, or attack from their enemies. The few nonreligious holidays were those that had been observed in England, such as the monarch's birthday.

During the 18th century, colonial Americans gradually began to develop a secular, nonreligious history of their own. Benjamin Franklin, for example, diligently sought to buy memorabilia for the Philadelphia Library Society with the view toward collecting and safeguarding original examples of early colonial events and traditions. According to historian Russell Nye, "[T]he American colonies were gradually finding out that they possessed a history, and that it was worth recalling."[1]

Based on this history, America began to develop a ceremonial calendar of patriotic holidays. These holidays remained few in number and, as with other patriotic symbols such as the flag or the national monuments, evolved but slowly. Each holiday is designed to mark an especially noteworthy occasion in the history of the nation and to stimulate patriotic sentiment among the American people. The nation's ceremonial calendar encourages patriotism, reminds us of our national heritage and traditions, contributes to an understanding of the nature and character of America, and inspires us to live up to the ideals as expressed in the American Creed.

WASHINGTON'S AND LINCOLN'S BIRTHDAYS

While observance of Washington's birthday began well before his death, February 22 became the first truly national holiday only after he died. It is not surprising that Washington should be so honored. Not only was he venerated as a national hero, but it had long been a British tradition to observe the birthday of the British monarch. With such a precedent, Americans were quick to observe the birthday of the one who came closest to playing for Americans a similar symbolic role to that of the king of England.

Shortly after Washington died on December 14, 1799, Congress adopted a resolution establishing February 22, 1800, as a day of national mourning. The day was solemnly observed through the administration of President John Adams, but President Thomas Jefferson held no special ceremony on Washington's birthday. Perhaps this was because in his lifetime, Washington was closer to the Federalists, the political party that opposed Jefferson. Later, the birthday was even more casually observed and tended to be partisan in character as each of the political parties sought to claim Washington for their own and thereby bask in his reflected glory.

Washington's birthday is now a legal holiday in all states, but its observance is still rather informal. Some communities mark the occasion with speeches, parades, and other festivities. Students in most schools participate in appropriate commemorative activities in the form of class projects or schoolwide assemblies, usually prior to February 22, which is generally a school holiday.

In recent years, the day of the actual observance of Washington's birthday has been moved to the Monday nearest February 22, called Presidents' Day, in order to provide an opportunity for a three-day holiday weekend. In most cities Washington's birthday has become a major shopping day with shoppers diligently searching the stores for merchandise at reduced prices.

However casually they may be celebrated, holidays such as Washington's birthday contribute to American patriotism by providing an occasion to be reminded of our national past. Speaking at Washington's home at Mount Vernon in 1961 on the occasion of Washington's birthday, President John F. Kennedy said, "As in the past, this anniversary of the birth of the father of our country inspires us anew with the strength for today's challenges. The spirit of George Washington is a living tradition, so that even today he serves his country well."

The first formal observance of Lincoln's birthday was held in Washington, D.C., on February 12, 1866. However, it was not until 1891 when Lincoln's first vice president, Hannibal Hamlin, suggested that his birthday be made a national holiday, were any steps taken toward this end. Illinois, the state with which Lincoln is most closely associated although he was not born there, was the first to do so. Other states followed. Today, 17 states still do not observe Lincoln's birthday. Because of opposition from southern states, there is no federal recognition of Lincoln's birthday. Among the former Confederate states, only Tennessee has officially adopted Lincoln's birthday as a holiday.

If Washington is remembered as the "father of the country," Abraham Lincoln is remembered as the "Savior of the Union." Although Washington's birthday is observed in all states and Lincoln's is not, it is somehow the latter that generates a greater emotional outlet. It was due to growing sentiment that Lincoln's birthday be appropriately observed and that the

Lincoln Memorial was built. Lincoln's birthday is the springboard for such observances as Brotherhood Week and Black History Month. The latter are designed to encourage an end to racial and religious bigotry and to recognize the contributions of African-Americans to the nation's development.

Where Washington seems remote and distant, Lincoln seems warm and intimate. Lincoln's birthday observances provide opportunities for a more personal identification with a president who had been assassinated. While Washington represents the triumph of a natural aristocracy based on talent, ability, and integrity, Lincoln represents the rise from a log cabin to the White House. More dramatically than Washington, Lincoln embodies the American Creed: he symbolizes America as the "land of opportunity," the "home of democracy," and the "cradle of liberty."

We have not given up on Washington by any means, but he seems beyond our reach and perhaps no longer speaks to us as an expression of America's role at home and abroad. Lincoln we can better understand. But is his voice fading too? And, if so, are there other voices, new symbols, that better express the national mood and better capture the meaning of America for today's Americans?

Although Washington remains a hero, today we are inclined to forget that however much he was honored in his own time, he was also much reviled and even hated by some. He had his share of enemies and was not unfamiliar with widespread personal abuse. Abraham Lincoln, too, admired by many in his own day and still revered by most in our own, was much criticized as president. Some members of the press in those days, for example, referred to him as a baboon. Birthday celebrations tend to gloss over these aspects of the lives of American heroes, but they also demonstrate that in America no one is above criticism, that patriotism does not mean servility, that to love one's country does not require worship of any one person or party.

Independence Day

John Adams once wrote to his wife, Abigail:

> *The Second of July, 1776 will be the most memorable epoch in the history of America. I am apt to believe that it will be celebrated by succeeding generations as the great anniversary festival. It ought to be commemorated as the day of deliverance, by solemn acts of devotion to God Almighty. It ought to be solemnized with pomp and parade, with shows, games and sports, guns, bells, bonfires and illuminations, from one end of this continent to the other, from this time forward for evermore.*

Adams was not entirely correct. Although Independence Day has been celebrated as he suggested, the day of its observance is July 4, not July 2, as he thought it would be. On July 2, the Declaration of Independence was agreed upon in principle by the Second Continental Congress, but it was not until July 4 that the Declaration was formally adopted. It took some time to get all 51 signatures on the document. By the time the deed was done, it was evident that the War of Independence would be long and painful and that England would not easily give up its 13 colonies. Thus, it is to the credit of the signers of the Declaration of Independence that they were neither thwarted nor discouraged by the initial setbacks on the fields of battle.

A year later, on July 4, 1777, Independence Day was celebrated in Philadelphia essentially as John

A horseback rider carries a flag during a July Fourth parade in Grants, New Mexico. Independence Day brings out the patriotism in many Americans.

Adams thought it should, with fireworks and bonfires, bells and cannons, speeches and parades, games and athletic contests. Music for the celebration of the first Independence Day was provided by mercenary Hessian soldiers who, having fought for pay in the service of the British, were in effect American prisoners of war. And there were some who complained that the celebration was too noisy and too frivolous, while others objected to the rowdyism that led to broken windows. But Independence Day became, almost at once, a national holiday.

In 1788, Independence Day was celebrated in Philadelphia with particular enthusiasm because it was then that the U.S. Constitution was finally ratified. John Adams and Thomas Jefferson both died on July 4, 1826, the date marking the fiftieth anniversary of the Declaration of Independence. Five years later on July 4, the fifth U.S. president, James Monroe, died. These deaths of some of the Founding Fathers on the official day of the nation's founding seemed to punctuate what Americans had long felt, that in the birth of the nation may be discerned the hand of God.

As the nation expanded and as Americans moved westward into Kentucky and Ohio, and later into the territory acquired from France in the Louisiana Purchase, it was natural that they should take the Fourth of July celebrations with them. Meriwether Lewis and William Clark, joint leaders of the expedition that initially explored the vast Louisiana Purchase at the request of President Jefferson, observed Independence Day on the trail with "a sumptuous dinner of fat saddles of venison."[2] And, in a journey sponsored by the American Board for Foreign Missions, Marcus Whitman and his wife, who in 1836 led the first party to cross the Rockies that included women, preferred to kneel down and, with Bible and flag, dedicate Oregon Territory as "the home of American mothers and the church of Christ."[3]

Special interest groups, such as antislavery crusaders and temperance advocates (those opposed to liquor consumption), sometimes tried to use the day to promote their own causes. At times, the celebrations of Independence Day became very partisan with rival celebrations by political parties in the same community. No other national holiday, however, has triggered as much patriotism or as great a show of unity and loyalty as has the Fourth of July. "The anniversary," Daniel Webster declared, "animates, and gladdens, and unites all American hearts. On other days of the year we may be party men, indulging in controversies, more or less important to the public good . . . but today we are Americans all and nothing but Americans."[4]

Central to the observance of the Fourth of July are parades and speeches. Historian Merle Curti studied July 4 oratory with special emphasis on the first 80 years of the Republic. His conclusion was:

> *Independence Day oration, for all its bombast and platitudes, epitomizes the whole pattern of American patriotic thought and feeling. Even when it was quickly forgotten, even when in their daily lives the men who had delivered it and the men who had listened to it forthwith indulged in profit making in public office, in outsmarting the government, in defying the national laws, in laboring for the advantage of state, section and class, the Fourth of July oration was still an invitation to patriotism and to an inspiration for loyalty to the nation.*[5]

Traditionally, Curti noted, "Independence Day oratory began with a recital of American history . . . and traced the hand of God at every point, emphasized the love of liberty of the early Americans, described the events leading up to the Revolution . . . glorified the heroism of the struggle for independence, expressed reverence for Revolutionary leaders, urged the importance of attacking existing problems in their spirit, took pride in the amazing material and social progress of the country, and expressed loyalty to the nation and faith in the future."[6] Today, the oratory is more varied. Because speaking styles have changed, speeches are less florid than they once were. There is perhaps more cynicism, an aspect of patriotism that Alexis de Tocqueville, the French sojourner in America during the 1830s, recognized and called "this irritable patriotism of the Americans."[7] That irritation is often evident in the oratory of Independence Day as minorities and other interest groups try to identify their views with the ideals for which the nation stands. Thus, there are speeches on behalf of women's rights, civil rights for African-Americans, Hispanics, Native Americans, and other racial minorities, and the unfinished business of the nation in caring for the poor, the hungry, and the homeless. Often, in recognition of America's global leadership, common cause is made with peoples struggling for independence in the less-developed regions of the world or, as in more recent years, with the people fighting in Bosnia or Croatia.

THANKSGIVING

Thanksgiving is a day of giving thanks for the blessings of health, life, security, serenity, bounty, family, and peace. The first Thanksgiving in the New World was observed by the Pilgrims in 1621. And in 1623, after an unusually severe winter during which the food supply had fallen dangerously low, Governor William Bradford proclaimed a day of Thanksgiving since the Lord had answered the prayers of the colony for a bountiful harvest. In a proclamation he declared:

> *TO ALL YE PILGRIMS: Inasmuch as the great Father has given us this year an abundant harvest of Indian corn, wheat, beans, squashes and garden vegetables, and has made the forests to abound with game and the sea with fish and clams, and inasmuch as He has protected us from the ravages of the savages, has spared us from pestilence and disease, has granted us freedom to worship God according to the dictates of our own conscience, now, I your magistrate, do proclaim that all ye Pilgrims, with your wives and little ones, do gather at ye meeting house, on ye hill, between the hours of 9 and 12 in the day time, on Thursday, November 19th of the year of our Lord one thousand and six hundred and twenty-three, and in the third year since ye Pilgrims landed on ye Pilgrim Rock, there to listen to ye pastor, and render thanksgiving to ye Almighty God for his blessing.*

After the United States declared its independence from England, the observances of Thanksgiving continued sporadically at the discretion of each state and local community. The idea of a uniform national day of thanksgiving was slow in coming.

George Washington proclaimed November 29, 1789, a day of national thanksgiving for having achieved a national union under a strong Constitution. Only John Adams and James Madison identified thanksgiving days, and they chose days in April, May, and September. Thomas Jefferson was consistently opposed to the holiday during the two terms of his administration on the grounds that it violated the principle of the separation of church and state.

That the nation now has a single day for the observance of Thanksgiving is due to the efforts of Sara

Josepha Hale, the editor of the then popular magazine *Godey's Lady's Book*. In 1846, she began a 17-year campaign for a national day of thanksgiving. "We have few holidays," she said. "Thanksgiving like the Fourth of July should be considered a national festival and observed by all people."[8] In her last editorial she wrote:

> *Can we not then . . . establish our yearly Thanksgiving as a permanent American National Festival which shall be celebrated on the last Thursday in November in every State of the Union? Indeed, it has been nearly accomplished. For the last twelve or fourteen years the States have made approaches to this unity. In 1859 thirty States held their Thanksgiving Festival on the same day—the last Thursday in November. It was also celebrated that year on board several of the American fleets—ships in the Indian Ocean, the Mediterranean, and on the Brazil station, by the Americans in Berlin at our Prussian Embassy, in Paris, and in Switzerland, and American Missionaries have signified their readiness to unite in the Festival if it should be established on a particular day that can be known as the American Thanksgiving. Then in every quarter of the globe our nationality would be recognized in connection with our gratitude to the Divine Giver of all our blessings. The pious and loving thought that every American was joining in heart with the beloved family at home and with the church to which he belongs would thrill his soul with the purest feelings of patriotism and the deepest emotions of thankfulness for his religious enjoyment.*

On October 3, 1863, in the midst of the Civil War, Abraham Lincoln issued his Thanksgiving Proclamation, making it a national holiday observed, as Sarah Josepha Hale had wished, on the last Thursday of November. With some flexibility, this has been the

This painting by Jean L. G. Ferris depicts the first Thanksgiving.

date of Thanksgiving since that time. In his proclamation Lincoln took note of the Civil War. He said:

> *In the midst of a Civil War of unequaled magnitude and severity . . . peace has been preserved with all nations, order has been maintained, the laws have been respected, and harmony has prevailed everywhere except in the theater of military conflict. . . . I do, therefore, invite my fellow citizens in every part of the United States, and also those who are at sea or those who are sojourning in for-*

eign lands, to set apart and observe the last Thursday of November next as a day of thanksgiving and praise to our beneficent Father who dwelleth in the heavens.

It is not clear whether turkey, cranberry sauce, and pumpkin pie—the staples of the modern Thanksgiving meal—were part of the early Thanksgivings, but they may have been. During the 19th century, Thanksgiving was observed with more religious ceremony than it is today, and in some communities children of the poor would dress in costumes and beg for fruit, vegetables, and pennies. In Plymouth, Massachusetts, on the site of Plymouth Colony a reenactment of the first Thanksgiving is presented. In many large cities, the day is marred or marked by commercialism. In New York City, for example, a huge parade that has been sponsored by a large department store since 1924 ushers in the Christmas shopping season.

Despite its commercial aspects, Thanksgiving Day offers an opportunity to remember the Pilgrim forebears of the nation, the Puritans, Plymouth Colony, the Mayflower, the Mayflower Compact. It creates an opportunity to remember the helpfulness of the Indian Squanto and the activities immortalized by Henry Wadsworth Longfellow in "The Courtship of Miles Standish." Thanksgiving is a national holiday and is shared by people of all races, recent immigrants and those whose families have been here for many years. But it also gives us all a chance to "speak for ourselves" as we give thanks for the country and what most have been able to accomplish under its protection.

Memorial and Veterans Days

Memorial Day, once called Decoration Day, is observed on May 30; Veterans Day, once called Armistice Day, is observed on November 11. These are patriotic holidays designed to honor America's war dead. Both days are occasions on which we, as a nation and as individuals and families, remember those in the armed forces who gave their lives for their country.

Decoration Day began obscurely toward the end of the Civil War. In 1966, Waterloo, New York, was legally recognized by Congress and the president as the community in which the commemoration began. Despite this official recognition, in a real sense the patriotic holiday may be said to have evolved rather than been proclaimed. For example, in 1866 the women of Columbus, Mississippi, decorated with flowers the graves of Confederate and Union soldiers alike who had fallen during the Battle of Shiloh (April 6 and 7, 1862). The *New York Herald* paid tribute to the women of Mississippi, who had "shown themselves impartial" in remembering the dead of both sides.

In 1868, Major J. A. Logan encouraged the observation of Decoration Day and specified May 30 as the day for decorating military graves. Why May 30 was chosen as a day to remember the Civil War dead is unclear although it does approximate the date of the surrender of the last Confederate army on May 26, 1865. In his order to the Grand Army of the Republic calling for the observance, Major Logan said, "Let no ravages of time testify in coming generations that we have forgotten, as a people, the cost of a free and undivided Republic."

Memorial Day tributes have taken place at Arlington National Cemetery near Washington, D.C., and at Civil War battlefield cemeteries, such as Gettysburg, Pennsylvania. In 1938, at the 75th anniversary of the Battle of Gettysburg, 1,800 Civil War veterans and an audience of 100,000 people joined in remembering the Civil War dead. On Memorial Day, 1958, one unidentified soldier from World War II and one from the Korean War were placed in the Tomb of the Unknown Soldier.

Memorial Day speeches typically take Civil War heroes as points of departure, and special emphasis is given to Abraham Lincoln, a war casualty through assassination. That the Civil War was a war between brothers and sisters is often emphasized. In some southern states tribute is paid to Confederate president Jefferson Davis and sometimes dates other than May 30 are used to honor Confederate war dead.

In recent years, Memorial Day has become a less somber occasion. The holiday generally is regarded as the official opening of the summer vacation season, and at Indianapolis, Indiana, the famous five-hundred-mile race of speeding cars is watched by thousands and, via television, viewed by millions. Is this an expression of American patriotism? Well, why not? Memorial Day was developed as a means of bringing us together, and to the extent that such activities bring families together and encourage wholesome activities, perhaps the holiday is achieving the goal for which it was created.

November 11 became Armistice Day because on that day the Germans signed the armistice ending World War I. A cease-fire along the entire western front in Europe was ordered for 11:00 A.M. the same day. In his Armistice Day proclamation of 1919, President Woodrow Wilson said, "To us in America the reflections of Armistice Day will be filled with solemn pride in the heroism of those who died in the country's service and with gratitude for the victory, both because of the thing from which it has freed us and because of the opportunity it has given America to show her sympathy with peace and justice in the councils of the nation."

The chief observance of Veterans Day takes place in the largest of America's national cemeteries, Arlington Cemetery. Once the estate of Robert E. Lee, the general who led the Confederate forces during the Civil War, it is now a burial ground for war heroes and others who gave their lives for their country. Thus, President John Fitzgerald Kennedy is buried here with an eternal flame marking his grave. Here also lies the Tomb of the Unknown Soldier. On November 11, 1921, at precisely 11:00 A.M. the body of an unknown soldier was lowered into this grave. President Warren G. Harding asked that flags be flown at half-staff and that silent tribute be paid the unknown soldier and all the American dead of World War I. The tomb consists of a 50-ton block of Colorado marble containing the legend: "Here rests in honored glory an American soldier known but to God." Army privates, rotating every hour, take turns guarding the tomb.

Organizations of veterans, such as the American Legion and the Veterans of Foreign Wars, try to keep alive the memory of those who have died in America's wars and take the lead in the commemorative ceremonies that take place throughout the nation. Veterans Day is marked, as are other patriotic holidays, by parades in which veterans of recent conflicts take part and are honored. Honoring the Vietnam War veterans has proved to be a special problem inasmuch as no victory followed their sacrifice. Although there was considerable controversy over the monument erected in belated recognition of their heroism, as the years go by they seem to be gaining in stature in the public mind, and vetrans of the Vietnam War more readily take part in activities which honor all the men and women who have served their country during wartime.

Case Study:
Reverend Martin Luther King Jr. Day

Taylor Branch, a biographer of Martin Luther King Jr.,[9] believes that there "was always a special kind of patriotism" about his speeches.[10] Who else could bring people of all races to their feet by quoting from "My Country 'Tis of Thee?" as he did in August 1963, to more than 250,000 whites and blacks in the march on Washington, when at the Lincoln Memorial he declared, "My country 'tis of thee, sweet land of liberty, of thee I sing, Land where my fathers died, land of the pilgrims' pride, from every mountainside, let freedom ring." In exercising his leadership in securing the "blessings of liberty" for African-Americans he called upon America to live up to the American Creed. "When the architects of our republic wrote the magnificent words of the Constitution and Declaration of Independence, they were signing a promissory note to which every American was to fall heir. This note was a promise that all men would be guaranteed the inalienable rights of life, liberty, and the pursuit of happiness."

As a result of his leadership and inspiration, Martin Luther King Jr.'s birthday became a national holiday in record time. King was assassinated on April 4, 1968, in Memphis, Tennessee, by James Earl Ray, an escaped convict. In 1980, the rules of the House of Representatives were suspended and the legislation to make King's birthday a national holiday passed by a vote of 338 to 90. In the Senate the bill was placed on a fast track and was passed by a vote of 78 to 22. President Ronald Reagan reluctantly signed the bill, and a new national holiday was launched.

Although the gears of government were greased so that King's birthday could swiftly become a national holiday, a number of controversies lingered just beneath the surface. Some people felt that it was simply premature to make King's birthday a national holiday. After all, it had taken 80 years for George Washington, the "father of the country," to be so recognized and Abraham Lincoln was never federally recognized. King's life, despite his achievements and the honor of winning the Nobel Peace Prize, had not, in the eyes of some, withstood the judgment of history.

Ironically, the holiday was adopted during the Reagan administration, when there were significant attempts to scale back legislation designed to improve voting rights and economic opportunities for minorities. Thus, in the minds of African-Americans the proposal to make King's birthday a national holiday was an empty gesture and an attempt to assuage their feelings so as to make the distasteful medicine go down a bit better. Nevertheless, African-Americans pressed forward to make King's birthday a national holiday while they still could and used the opportunity to keep up the pressure so that recent gains in civil rights and economic opportunities would not be eroded.

Once the holiday was established, there was little enthusiasm in Congress to provide money for staff and office space so that plans for the first observance could be made.

The Federal Bureau of Investigation, under its long-time head J. Edgar Hoover, had consistently spied on King. Hoover felt that King's personal life was too unconventional to merit American adulation. Some senators, such as Jesse Helms, believed, as did Hoover, that King was a communist sympathizer. When President Ronald Reagan was asked whether King was a communist sympathizer, he gave a rather noncommittal reply. "We'll see, won't we," he said, meaning when all of King's papers were made available.

King was an agitator. That is, he fought for civil rights for African-Americans and fought against the Vietnam War. In doing so, he made numerous enemies among those who were against what he wanted to achieve.

Although King was popular among African-Americans, he

On the first national observance of Martin Luther King Jr. Day in 1986, Vice President George Bush (left) and South African Bishop Desmond Tutu (right) join Coretta Scott King during a wreath-laying ceremony at the crypt of the slain civil rights leader.

was not uniformly popular among black leaders. Many were opposed to the direction in which he wanted to go. Some were against his use of Gandhi-influenced nonviolent techniques to create change.[11] Others were simply jealous of his leadership role and hoped to replace him.

That these controversies did not throw enough sand into the

machinery of government to slow it down or grind it to a halt is, in itself, remarkable. Questions about King's character, views, and lifestyle were muted as the government mechanism to establish the birthday of Martin Luther King Jr. as a national holiday moved ahead with unaccustomed speed. How does one explain it? Former U.S. senator and 1996 Republican presidential candidate Robert Dole once called King "a drum major for justice and peace." African-Americans saw King leading them to equality. Whites saw King leading the nation toward racial harmony. Thus, whites and blacks alike recognized in King a person who helped move the nation closer to the ideals of the American Creed. Because he had done so, they were prepared to forgive his shortcomings.

But in view of this, just what is the meaning of King's birthday? While all other birthdays of great Americans are commemorated because of their achievements, "What makes King's birthday different from every other national holiday is that it is part of the unfinished social movement it is meant to honor."[12] His birthday reminds us that the march for justice remains incomplete.

America's patriotic holidays are symbols that help "to draw all people together to emphasize their similarities and common heritage, to minimize their differences and to contribute to their thinking, feeling and acting alike."[13] These patriotic holidays allow Americans to express common sentiments, but in doing so, they also provide Americans the opportunity to express thoughts about themselves and about their country.

America is a diverse and complex land and was so at its very birth. Is it to be wondered that its patriotic holidays are observed in diverse ways? America's diversity and complexity are America's strengths, so patriotic holidays are often used as occasions to blame as well as to praise, to exult as well as to criticize. The holidays provide an opportunity for Americans to identify those times when America as a nation fell short of achieving the American Creed as well as those when it rose to the challenge. The unifying theme of America's patriotic holidays provide an umbrella under which Americans can take pride in the nation's accomplishments, can give voice to its shortcomings, while expressing their essential patriotism. The many ways in which the patriotic holidays are observed provides more than just a hint that American patriotism is fragile and needs nurturing. It is to that theme to which we turn in the final chapter.

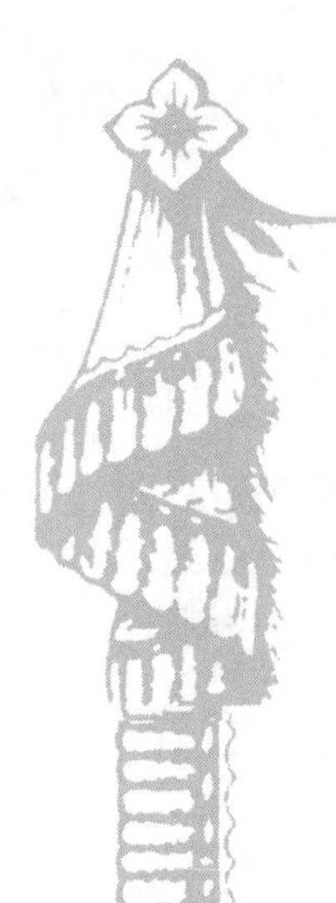

Seven

Are Modern Americans Patriotic?

And so, my fellow Americans: Ask not what your country can do for you—ask what you can do for your country.

— Inaugural address of John Fitzgerald Kennedy, 1961

Patriotism in a democracy is as fragile as it is complex. It is not knee-jerk love of country, nor blind obedience to a political leader or popular hero. It is not "our country right or wrong," as Stephen Decatur, an early American naval hero declared, but rather as Carl Schurz, a German immigrant who served as a

Union general during the Civil War and as secretary of the interior during the Rutherford B. Hayes administration put it, "Our country right or wrong, when right to be kept right, when wrong to be put right."

When viewed in this tradition, American patriotism is neither unthinking nor narrowly defined. Just as "love thy neighbor as thyself" involves first self-love, without which one cannot love one's neighbor, so patriotism evokes first love for the land where one lives, without which one cannot love the lands where others live, one's global neighbors. Frances Wright, an early American feminist, in a speech on the Fourth of July in 1828, succinctly expressed this concept of American patriotism. She urged upon America a broader, and more inclusive concept of patriotism. After noting that the United States is a country "which is truly the home of all nations and in the veins of whose citizens flows the blood of every people on the globe," Wright went on to assert:

> *Patriotism, in the exclusive meaning, is surely not made for America. The very origin of the people is opposed to it. The institutions, in their principle militate against it. The day we are celebrating protests against it. It is for Americans, more especially, to nourish a nobler sentiment; one more consistent with their origin, and more conducive to their future improvement. It is for them more especially to know why they love their country; and to feel that they love it, not because it is their country, but because it is the palladium of human liberty—the favored scene of human improvement.*

Thus, American patriotism articulates a universal concern for "liberty and justice for all."

Is American Patriotism Fragile?

If by fragile one means that American patriotism is brittle and is, therefore, easily broken the answer is clearly, "No." If, on the other hand, one means that American patriotism is delicate and needs to be carefully cultivated and cannot be taken for granted then the answer is equally clearly, "Yes." It is in the latter sense that we will examine selected aspects of American patriotism today.

In the United States, patriotism is especially delicate in that our federal system calls forth also devotion to one of 50 states and to a region, such as New England or the Deep South, and to areas that have abiding distinctive traditions of their own, such as the Hispanic Southwest. In a mobile society in which people move about freely from one geographic location to another without hindrance or internal security clearances, the ties that bind one to a region, to a state, and especially to a nation become loose and ill defined.

Making the development and expression of American patriotism ever more difficult is our tradition of relatively generous immigration policies. How does a nation develop a unified patriotism in a people whose roots go back to many distant lands? How much of the heritage of the land where immigrants were born ought to be erased and how much ought they be encouraged to retain? To what degree can those whose ancestors were forced to these shores as enslaved men and women be expected to develop ties of patriotism to the nation?

American patriotism has been able to overcome many of these diverse stresses and strains because there was a vast and vacant land to be explored, settled, and cultivated. The idea of a vast land whose soil needed to be tilled, whose forests needed to be cleared, whose minerals needed to be mined, whose factories needed to be made productive, whose cities needed to be built and rebuilt as they expanded, molded the American character, transcended local loyalties, and contributed to devotion to the nation.

The perception, as well as the reality, of a vast frontier suggested that there was an overarching mission that united pioneer and city dweller alike in a common loyalty to the country as a whole. Because of the availability of free or nearly free land, Americans could dream of an abundant future, which fueled the fires of American patriotism and encouraged unabashed loyalty to its symbols. With the end of the frontier, and in our age of less rather than more, can patriotism flourish where abundance may no longer be available? If, as some fear, tomorrow may not be better than today, whither American patriotism?

American patriotism is fragile because the United States was founded on the idea of equal opportunity rather than on the basis of a homogeneous people. "Everywhere else in the world," wrote political observer Theodore White, "politics dominates culture. Not so in America. Americans are not a people like the French, Germans, or Japanese whose genes have been mixing with kindred genes for thousands of years. Americans are held together only by ideas, the clashing ideas of opportunity and equality—and as it were by a culture of hope."[1] What happens to love of country when one person's opportunity clashes with another's search for equality?

Patriotism in America is fragile because what one person believes is in the very best interests of the nation may be flatly contradicted by the views of another patriot who thinks entirely differently. Historian Merle Curti observed, "As long as conflicting interests within the United States struggle for existence and for power, so long will conflicting conceptions of patriotism continue to flourish."[2] The paradox of American patriotism is how to love America as its people search in diverse ways to achieve, insofar as it is possible, all that is expressed in the American Creed.

During America's 1976 bicentennial, Americans paid homage to Washington, Jefferson, and Adams—those whom Abraham Lincoln in the Gettysburg Address of 1862 called our "Founding Fathers." Yet, writing in the bicentennial issue of *Public Interest*, the sociologist Daniel Bell feared that most Americans no longer believed in Americanism in the original meaning of that term. What made America "exceptional," he said, was that Americanism meant "providing individual opportunity, safeguarding liberties and expanding the standard of living."[3] Do people still, he wondered, "identify achievement and equality with pride in nation or patriotism?"[4]

Because of the divisions brought about in our society during the 1970s by the Vietnam War, the Watergate scandal, and an economic roller coaster that included hyperinflation followed by unemployment at the highest levels since the Great Depression of the 1930s, Bell's concern that Americans were less committed to the unique qualities of America was also expressed by others. In July 1979, President Jimmy Carter declared that the nation was experiencing a crisis of confidence that strikes at the very heart and soul and spirit of our national will. America, he said, "was losing [its] confidence in the future [and] beginning to close the door on its past."

Surely American patriotism is sturdier than Carter and Bell supposed. These dire forebodings that

America had lost its soul, that Americans no longer care about their country, appear to be vast overstatements as the following data suggest.

ARE AMERICANS PATRIOTIC?

In a survey conducted in 1981, some Americans responded to questions about their patriotism:

> Question: *How proud are you to be an American?*
>
> Answer: *Seventy-eight percent described themselves as being "extremely proud" and only two percent as "not proud at all."*
>
> Question: *Do you think the United States has a special role to play in the world today or is it pretty much like other countries?*
>
> Answer: *Eighty percent nationally insisted that the country occupied a special place, while only 15 percent said the United States was simply another country.*
>
> Question: *What are you proudest about America?*
>
> *Answer: More than two-thirds said they were proudest of freedom or liberty.*[5]

Nine out of ten questioned believed that "the United States [is] the very best place to live." Fifty-six percent believed that the best is still ahead for the United States. These responses were not confined to a single group of Americans. Eighty-eight percent of the young thought this country was the very best place to live, as did 95 percent of those over 65. Ninety-three percent of those earning $5,000 a year felt this way, as did 92 percent of those earning over $25,000. Ninety-four percent of whites thought that the United States was the very best place to live as did 86 percent of blacks.

Case Study: The Alamo

What happens to American patriotism when history is revised and seemingly sacred myths are "debunked?" A good illustration of this is the Alamo. By 1835 some 30,000 Americans had moved to Texas, which was then a province of Mexico. To free themselves from what they regarded as limitations upon their liberty, Texans declared their independence. Under their own flag, the Lone Star, Texans proceeded to defend themselves against the Mexican dictator, General Santa Anna. On February 23, 1836, Santa Anna and his 6,000 troops laid siege to the Alamo, a fort in San Antonio, Texas, where 187 Texans defended themselves until March 6, when all the defenders of the Alamo were massacred. The commander William Travis was killed. James Bowie, the inventor of the knife that bears his name and known throughout the Southwest as "the genuwine [*sic*] Arkansas toothpick," was shot in the back as he lay sick in bed. Davy Crockett, with coonskin cap on head and rifle in hand, was found dead, his body riddled with bullets. As if this were not enough, 400 American volunteers from nearby Goliad who had come to the aid of the defenders of the Alamo were brutally slaughtered after agreeing to lay down their arms. Little wonder then that a popular ballad of the day went: "For every wound and every thrust / On prisoners dealt by hand accurst / A Mexican shall bite the dust / Remember the Alamo!"

With that cry ringing in their ears, Texans, under the leadership of Sam Houston, defeated about 1200 Mexicans and captured Santa Anna at the Battle of San Jacinto on April 21, 1836. Houston became president of an independent Texas.

But what if the story did not go quite this way?

According to historians using new evidence, the Alamo was defended by scoundrels, not heroes. Davy Crockett tried to

The Alamo is situated in downtown San Antonio. The controversy over whether the Alamo defenders were heroes or scoundrels continues.

surrender. William Barret Travis, under the influence of mercury, a medicine he was taking to combat venereal disease, was nearly crazy. Sam Houston was an opium addict. Moreover, Jim Bowie was not at the Alamo seeking to win independence for Texas but was simply trying to hide a hoard of silver and gold that he had stolen from Apaches he had butchered.

In view of these revelations, should the Alamo continue to be regarded as a sacred shrine for patriotic Americans? If not, what happens to the city of San Antonio and the thousands who prosper from the influx of tourists? Is the Alamo best remembered as an heroic battle of Texans against tyranny or the triumph of imperialism and racism over Mexicans and Indians? Travis had appealed for help "in the name of liberty, of patriotism and everything dear to the American character," but was the Alamo merely a defense of land illegally grabbed from Mexico? Which of the versions should Americans remember: John Wayne's movie *The Alamo* (1960) in which Crockett and his fellow defenders die heroically, or the historians' story of the Alamo with all its warts showing?

In 1984, when asked about the obligation of young men to serve in the military, 83 percent declared that this obligation was very important while only 2 percent denied the obligation.[6] In a CBS/*New York Times* poll taken in November 1985, 97 percent of Americans asked said "they were very proud or somewhat proud to be an American."[7] In a survey taken in 1991, 87 percent of blacks declared, "I am very patriotic," while 89 percent of whites made the same declaration.[8]

At times Americans may be disenchanted with their leaders. They may feel, even rather often, that their leaders do not know what they are doing or wonder whether they can be trusted. Americans have, in various polls, indicated dissatisfaction with the performance of the nation or the skill of its leaders.

Despite the disillusionment brought on by the Vietnam War, the Watergate scandals, or the humiliation of America when in 1979 President Carter could not obtain the release of 52 American hostages held by Iran, patriotism has not been seriously eroded. "Fervid displays of patriotism have been customary in the United States since the early 1800s. There is no evidence of any recent decline; the celebrations marking the successive bicentennials of the Declaration of Independence and the Constitution, and the centennial of the Statue of Liberty, were extraordinarily enthusiastic."[9] In general, "Americans haven't withdrawn support for Americanism or altered their basic attachment to the nation and its institutions."[10]

In 1981, the political scientist Richard Reeves followed the technique of Alexis de Tocqueville and took a journey around the country in an attempt to assess the depth of American patriotism through interviews with ordinary people, some of whom had not fared well at the hands of America. De Tocqueville had spent nine months traveling around the country, conducting interviews, and making observations. What he found among Americans was what he called an "irritable patriotism" in which Americans were well aware of their country's shortcomings but were reluctant to let others criticize it. In his three years of travel, Richard Reeves found a parallel outlook.

In Alaska, Reeves interviewed a Tlingit Indian who had been a marine recruit in San Diego. The man explained how, during the course of his training, he lost half his hearing and most of his teeth and that was called "Nigger" by the drill instructors. "How do you feel about being an American after that?"

"I love it," he said. "I'm proud to be an American. This is the greatest country on earth."

A black policeman in Detroit declared that despite

discrimination, "It's a hell of a country—the best." A white woman in Ontario, California, who had just lost her job told Reeves, "I'm proud to be an American. This is a wonderful place." Richard Reeves concluded: "There is, Americans told me 150 years later, true greatness here. Those ideas, those promises, that union of generations, those generous passions—they are our birthright."[11]

Ebbs and Flows of American Patriotism

According to John Schaar, a political scientist who has written movingly about American patriotism, love of country has two faces. One face is that of the American whose patriotism is strident and militant and for whom national greatness and superiority are everything. This group hears patriotism in military marches, such as "The Stars and Stripes Forever." The other face is gentler. This group prefers the strains of "America the Beautiful." Patriotism to them is rooted in the love of the ideals for which the nation stands.[12] The barometer of American patriotism has fluctuated between these two views.

In America the nature of patriotism has varied with the values and styles of the period. Historian Dixon Wecter describes the period from Patrick Henry (1736–99) to Daniel Webster (1782–1852) as the "Silver Age" of American patriotism. It was characterized he said, by an oratory and grandiosity in which "one could scarcely see the hero from the incense."[13] From about 1850 to the Civil War, patriotism was sentimental in nature as "taught by McGuffey's readers and by children's lives of the great."[14] Patriotism during this period was based on devotion to homely virtues of simple goodness, family, honesty, decency, obedience to parents, and devotion to God as well as to country.

During the Civil War new giants, such as Lincoln, Lee, and Grant, were elevated to national heroes. The war itself was an important test of American patriotism. The noble Lee felt that patriotism meant that he had to return to Virginia to lead the Army of Northern Virginia in a cause that he knew could not be long sustained.

No one spelled out the values for which the nation stood more effectively than President Abraham Lincoln in the Gettysburg Address, the Emancipation Proclamation, and his second inaugural address. The Emancipation Proclamation enlisted the patriotism of those who favored the immediate end to slavery (abolitionists), but many a Union soldier questioned whether he was prepared to give his life to free slaves.

Because one could "buy" a waiver of conscription for $300 and thereby pay for a substitute, the Civil War was sometimes dubbed "a rich man's war but a poor man's fight." While soldiers were rallying around the flag, despite their misgivings and reservations, and fighting for "union forever," contractors North and South sold shoddy goods and defective weaponry to the military. Nevertheless, patriotism withstood the test of the Civil War as Lincoln made the Northern cause a holy one. In the Gettysburg Address, he sought to enlist the devotion of the North to the "honored dead." In his second inaugural he called upon the nation to "finish the work we are in . . . with malice toward none and with charity for all."

Following the Civil War, patriotism had a highly materialistic content. This was an age of building: railroads, dams, and factories sprung up across the country. National grandeur seemed at low ebb as people measured their well-being by their possessions. In

1890, the frontier was declared to exist no longer; manifest destiny as a national goal appeared to have been achieved. Overseas adventures proved to be but a flirtation for America, and as World War I approached Woodrow Wilson needed to stir the nation to action and to speak to its people in a nobler language.

Encouragement of patriotism enabled the nation to prepare for war, if need be. The sinking of the *Lusitania* in 1916 spurred the movement to get ready to fight Germany and the Central Powers. "I didn't raise my boy to be a soldier," may have been the song of pacifists—those who opposed all war for whatever purpose—but Wilson tempered America's preparedness for war with the theme that it was "the duty of Americans to champion throughout the world the principles of order, decency, peace and freedom."[15] Patriotic zeal was sometimes excessive: Americans of German descent were harassed, the German language could not be taught in school, and German books were burned. But during the war years, it was Wilson's idealism rather than anti-German excesses that dominated expressions of patriotism.

Not so, however, once the war was over. Patriotism itself took on a bad name. Twin forces contributed to the postwar decline in patriotic sentiment. On the one hand, cynicism set in, and on the other, patriotism was debunked. Those who went to fight in France were deemed fools. Anyone who gave an arm or leg for his country was, a poster proclaimed, "a sucker."[16] Some historians wrote about impersonal forces of history and devalued the role of heroes in the making of America. The onset of the Great Depression in 1929 gave impetus to the idea of the "class struggle" in which history was thought to be nothing more than a struggle between the rich and poor, between workers and their bosses.

Whitaker Chambers (at microphone) testifies before the House Un-American Activities Committee (HUAC) in August 1948. Beginning in 1938, the HUAC investigated organizations and individuals thought to be "un-American," particularly those purported to have ties to communism.

As if to counter this decline in patriotic emotion, there were others who sought to develop the concept of the "one hundred percent" American. One hundred percentism systematically repudiated the very ideals of the American Creed. Reformers, Roman Catholics, Jews, Native Americans, African-Americans, Hispanic-Americans, and new immigrants from eastern and southern Europe were subjected to a humiliation deep enough to question the very meaning of what Washington and Lincoln stood for.

Bigotry, racism, and censorship of speech and press were pressed into the service of a pseudopatriotism. Fear of communists, then variously described as Reds, Bolsheviks, or anarchists, led to raids by Attorney General A. Mitchell Palmer. The Fighting Quaker, as he was called, saw Reds wherever he looked. Violating or bypassing safeguards for freedom of expression, Palmer sought to imprison radicals or, in the case of those who were not citizens, to ship them abroad. Two hundred forty-nine suspected alien radicals were rounded up and deported. In his zeal, Palmer forgot that patriotism incorporates the right of dissent and that disagreement is not unpatriotic.

As World War II approached there was a new need to reunite the nation. It took a sneak attack on Pearl Harbor in Hawaii on December 7, 1941, to arouse the nation to the threat that Nazi Germany, fascist Italy, and Japan under Emperor Hirohito posed. America went about the task of winning World War II, "our good war," with less fanfare than accompanied World War I. There was a more realistic understanding of what sacrifices war required and more of a conviction that those sacrifices were necessary.

But when the war ended, patriotism was once again dealt the double blow of cynicism and extremism. Cynicism was expressed by those who felt that patriotism is bunk and that making sacrifices for the nation is futile. Extremism took the form of ferreting out so-called un-American activities that were identified as such by those who sought to benefit from the national concern over the spread of communism by stifling dissent or cries for reform.

We were concerned after World War II, as were Americans in 1776, that America should somehow show the way. We Americans would show Europeans how to live in peace with one another. We would show less developed, or third-world, countries how to win independence, establish democratic government, develop a market economy, raise living standards, and promote human rights. But this innocence and idealism were short-lived. A cold war made genuine peace and mutual trust seem more distant than ever. The third-world countries, having overthrown old masters, were torn by internal, factional strife or ruled by dictators who imposed a harsh and uneasy peace. The shackles of colonialism had been severed, only to have new shackles self-imposed by homegrown despots. Traditional cultures clashed with technological cultures, as people sought futilely to find and cling to something they valued. Fear that atomic bombs in the hands of irresponsible nations could trigger a calamity that can scarcely be measured, now hangs over the relationships among states. The authority once wielded by the major global powers seems to be eroding as weak and irresponsible states whose leaders feel they have little to lose threaten to develop and use atomic weapons.

On December 26, 1991, the experiment with communism which began in 1917 in the Union of Soviet Socialist Republics ended in failure. America had won the cold war, but what would it or should it do with its victory?

Epilogue

The author John Gunther reminds us that the death of patriotism means the death of America. Yet we live in an age of the antihero and the antipatriot. The Pledge of Allegiance rarely touches our hearts, the flag seldom brings a lump to the throat, and the national anthem hardly ever quickens our pulse. And so we raise the question, "Can a society that mocks its patriotic symbols, fails to observe its patriotic holidays, and scorns its heroes, respond to the continuing crises of a changing world and nation?"

Patriotism may be said to be today's great American frustration. In simpler times, one put the flag on the lawn or in the window on the Fourth of July and other patriotic holidays. If the country appeared threatened, people more eagerly participated in demonstrations of patriotic zeal. If one had a son or daughter in the service, the flag was flown with even greater pride; it became a memorial for those families who had lost someone fighting for country.

Today we stand once again on the threshold of a redefinition of American patriotism. We need now, as never before in our history, the patriotism that provides national purpose and domestic tranquillity, and the conviction that there is something in our people, in our traditions, in our beliefs, and in short, in the American Creed, that is worth keeping and sharing. How may this be achieved?

1. Schools and colleges need to teach Americans how to be a part of the national community even as they are concerned with those among us who have suffered at America's hands. America has glorious traditions, but at times these get tarnished and there is no doubt that at times women, African-Americans, Hispanic-Americans, Native Americans, and other minorities have been dealt a bad hand. But in the attempt to be responsive to cultural differences and the needs of minorities, we need to find ways to encourage these groups to pull together rather than to engage in a zero-sum game in which progress for one means a loss for others and keeps them estranged from one another and from the nation as a whole. Writing in the op-ed page of the *New York Times*, Richard Rorty, a humanities professor at the University of Virginia, noted: "There is no incompatibility between respect for cultural differences and American patriotism."[1]
2. After a period during the 1920s when the gates were tightly shut to newcomers from abroad, America has once again become a nation of immigrants. How does the nation get those who bring their own memories to claim the Founding Fathers as their ancestors and America's history as their own? More than a century ago, Abraham Lincoln offered a partial answer. In a speech in Chicago shortly after Independence Day in 1858, Lincoln, who was not yet president, noted that half the people of his day had no ancestor who was present when the nation was born. How could these new citizens connect to the American

past? While new immigrants cannot trace their ancestry to the founding of the nation through ties of blood, Lincoln believed that children of enslaved men and women and new Americans would recognize that the principles of equal opportunity and self-government were meant for them as well. If one recognizes that the Founding Fathers were founders not so much of a nation as of a moral principle then they have a right to claim a relationship "as though they were the blood of the blood, and flesh of the flesh of the men" who wrote it. In this spirit, Chinese, Croatians, Iranians, African-Americans, Koreans, and others among us have a right to claim the founders of the republic as their ancestors.[2]

3. The true American patriot recognizes the tension that exists in patriotism. According to John Schaar, the patriot "loves one's own place and respect[s] the places of others."[3] Loyalty can keep alive this "noble tension" as he calls it. Because we love our country on the one hand we strive to improve it, and on the other we recognize that other people love their country as well and we respect them for it.

   In the early days of the Republic we looked to Europe for money to help us build our railroads and to invest in our industry and farmland, but today America is a donor nation. Not only do we reach out through governmental and nongovernmental agencies to help others in distress, but we export the American Creed as well. The Peace Corps, for example, not only provides underdeveloped nations with much-needed technical skill and competence but also has the benefit that those who join serve others as well as America by introducing them to our idealism and mission.

Given the nature of American patriotism Americans can understand with great clarity the yearning for independence of other nations. Thus we supported the movement for Greek independence in the 1830s, sympathized with the Irish in their struggle against England following World War I, and in general look with favor on the special relationship America has with the still relatively young nation of Israel.

Whereas Americans have learned to accept living in a multiethnic country, many people elsewhere have failed to. Thus, there are separatist movements today that threaten world peace. With the end of the cold war we see the rise of separatist movements among the ethnic groups of the former Soviet Union and the former Yugoslavia. Alsatians, Bretons, Scots, Corsicans, Basques, with greater or lesser intensity, remain unreconciled to ethnic pluralism. To the extent that America can show the way, it does a universal service in the interests of peace.

4. Perhaps the real danger in the loss of patriotism is the loss also of a sense of obligation to ourselves and to others. If we do not take pride in our country will we then take pride in ourselves and in our jobs? If we do not love our country will we then vote in numbers large enough to make representative government work? If we lack a sense of obligation to our country will we then also lack a sense of obligation to our family or our neighbors? If we desecrate the flag and trivialize our national holidays will we then erode our social, religious, economic. and political institutions?

These are the challenges of patriotism in a mature nation. How America responds will be up to the readers of this volume.

Source Notes

Prologue

1. Wilbur Zilensk, *Nation into State: The Shifting Symbolic Foundations of American Nationalism* (Chapel Hill: University of North Carolina Press, 1988), p. 224.
2. Quoted in Michael Kammen, *Mystic Chords of Memory: The Transformation of Tradition in American Culture* (New York: Knopf, 1991), p. 11.

Chapter One

1. Dixon Wecter, *The Hero in America* (New York: Scribners Sons, 1972), p. 2.
2. John Lukacs, *The Duel* (New York: Ticknor and Fields, 1991), p. 50.
3. Walter Lippman, *A Preface to Morals* (New York: Macmillan, 1929), pp. 156–57.
4. Hendrick Hertzberg, "What Is Patriotism," *Nation* (Vol. 253, No. 3, July 15, 1991), p. 98.
5. Morton Grodzins, *The Loyal and the Disloyal* (New York: World, 1966), p. 252.

Chapter Two

1. John Jay, *The Federalist Papers #2*, ed. Clinton Rossiter (New York: New American Library, 1961), p. 38.

2. Quoted in Russell Nye, *This Almost Chosen People* (Lansing: Michigan State University Press, 1966), p. 45.
3. Edward F. Humphrey, *Nationalism and Religion in America: 1774–1789* (New York: Russell and Russell, 1965), p. 5.
4. Ibid., p. 10.
5. Merle Curti, *Roots of American Loyalty* (New York: Russell and Russell, 1967), p. 53.
6. Ibid., p. 78.
7. Quoted in Humphrey, p.6.
8. Quoted in Theodore Lewis, *Sermons at Touro Synagogue* (New York: Simcha-Graphics Associates, 1980), p. xvii.
9. Alexis de Tocqueville, *Democracy in America*, vol. 1 (New York: Vintage Press, 1990), pp. 303–7, *passim*.
10. Quoted in Humphrey, p. 8
11. Shailer Matthews, *Patriotism and Religion* (New York: Macmillan, 1918), pp. 116–61, *passim*.
12. Quoted in Michael Kammen, p. 70.
13. Arthur Schlesinger Jr., "The Cult of Ethnicity, Good and Bad." *Time* 138, no. 1 (July 8, 1991), p. 21.
14. Quoted in Arthur Schlesinger Jr., *The Disuniting of America: Reflections on a Multicultural Society* (New York: Norton, 1992), p. 118.
15. Bicentennial Commission, *Writings of George Washington* (Washington, D.C.: U.S. Government Printing Office, 1934), p. 216.
16. Curti, p. 119.
17. Nye, p. 50.
18. Curti, p. 118.
19. Quoted in David H. Appel, ed., *An Album for Americans* (New York: Triangle, 1983), p. xiv.
20. The term comes from Jonathan Swift's novel *Gulliver's Travels*. It describes a race of brutes in human shape with degrading practices. In short, a rough, coarse, uncouth person.
21. Michel-Guillaume Jean de Crèvecoeur, "Letters from an American Farmer" (1782); quoted in Oscar Handlin, ed., *This Was America* (New York: Harper Torchbooks, 1949), p. 39. Had he been writing today, Crèvecoeur surely would have included women.

Chapter Three

1. Langston Hughes, "Democracy," in *Selected Poems of Langston Hughes* (New York: Knopf, 1970), p. 285.
2. Quoted in Gunnar Myrdal, *An American Dilemma: The Negro Problem and Modern Democracy* (New York: Harper and Row, 1964), p. 4.
3. Mary Antin, *The Promised Land* (Boston: Houghton Mifflin, 1912), p. 186.
4. Seymour Martin Lipset, *America As a New Nation* (New York: Basic Books, 1963), p. 15.
5. Dixon Wecter, p.2.

Chapter Four

1. Nye, p. 70.
2. Ibid., p. 65.
3. Quoted in Albert Matthews, "Brother Jonathan" in *The Colonial Society of Massachusetts: Transactions, 1900–1902*, vol. 7, pp. 115–16.
4. Ibid., pp. 118–19.
5. Curti, p. 142.
6. Maymie Kruthe, *What So Proudly We Hail: All about Our American Flag, Monuments and Symbols* (New York: Harper and Row, 1968), p. 51.
7. Ibid., p. 53.
8. Curti, p. 130.
9. Benjamin Franklin letter to Sarah Bache, January 26, 1786; quoted in Elinor Lander Horwitz, *The Bird, the Banner and Uncle Sam* (New York: Lippincott, 1976), p. 37.
10. Roger Butterfield in Milo Quaif, Melvin J. Weig, Roy E. Appleman, *The History of the United States Flag* (New York: Harper and Row), p.11.
11. Ibid.
12. Quoted in Richard Bernstein with Jerome Agel, *Amending America* (New York: Times Books, 1993), p. 1922.
13. Alan Brinkley, "The Saga of a National Love Affair" *New York Times*, July 1, 1990, sec. 4, p. 2.
14. Ibid.

15. For more on this subject *see* Caldwell Titcomb "Star Spangled Earache," *New Republic*, 193, no. 25 (December 16, 1985), pp. 11–12.

Chapter Five

1. Curti, p. 134.
2. Quoted in Kammen, pp. 163–64.
3. Lawrence Martin, "Women Fought at Bunker Hill," *New England Quarterly*, vol. 8, no. 4 (December 1935), pp. 478–79.
4. Richard Frothingham, *History of the Siege of Boston, and of the Battles of Lexington, Concord, and Bunker Hill* (New York: Da Capo, 1970), p. 359.
5. Quoted in George J. Olszewski, *A History of the Mall* (Washington, D.C.: Department of Interior, 1970), p. 15.
6. Ibid., p. 30.
7. Quoted in Paul Weinbaum, *Statue of Liberty* (Las Vegas, NV: Heritage of America, 1979), p. 13.
8. *See also* Gerald Leinwand, *Shall We Close the Open Door?* (New York: Franklin Watts, 1995).
9. Quoted in Colleen O'Connor with Peter McKillop and Nikki Greenberg, "Monumental Dispute," *Newsweek* (December 9, 1985), p. 27.
10. Ralph Barton Perry, "Uncle Sam and the Statue of Liberty," *Century Magazine*, 167 (February 1924), p. 164.
11. Quoted in Edward F. Conklin, ed., *The Lincoln Memorial* (Washington, D.C.: U.S. Government Printing Office, 1927), p. 15.
12. Ibid., p. 19.
13. Ibid., p. 81.
14. Quoted in James M. Mayo, *War Memorials As Political Landscape: The American Experience and Beyond* (New York: Praeger, 1988), p. 201.
15. Quoted in John Bodnar, *Remaking America: Public Memory, Commemoration and Patriotism in the Twentieth Century* (Princeton, N.J.: Princeton University Press, 1992, p. 7.

Chapter Six

1. Nye, p. 53.
2. Curti, p. 138.
3. Ibid.
4. Curti, p. 139.
5. Curti, p. 141.
6. Curti, p. 140.
7. Tocqueville, p. 244.
8. Ruth E. Finley, *The Lady of Godey's* (Philadelphia: Lippincott, 1931), p. 119.
9. Taylor Branch, *Parting the Waters* (New York: Simon and Schuster, 1988).
10. Taylor Branch, "Uneasy Holiday," *New Republic*, 194, no. 5 (February 3, 1986), p. 23.
11. Mohandas K. Gandhi was an Indian Hindu leader who preached resisting oppression through nonviolent methods.
12. "The March Goes On," *Nation*, 242, no. 4 (February 1, 1986), p. 99.
13. Grodzins, p. 61.

Chapter Seven

1. Theodore White, *America in Search of Itself* (New York: Harper and Row), 1982, p. 71.
2. Curti, p. 247.
3. Daniel Bell, "The End of American Exceptionalism," *Public Interest*, no. 41 (Fall 1975), p. 197.
4. Ibid., p. 207.
5. Everett Carl Ladd, "205 and Going Strong." *Public Opinion*, 4, no. 3, (June/July 1981), pp. 9–11.
6. Theodore Caplow, Howard M. Bahr, John Modell, and Bruce A. Chadwick, *Recent Social Trends in the United States, 1960-1990* (Frankfurt am Main, Germany: Campys Verlag, 1991), p. 562.
7. Quoted in Dennis A. Gilbert, *Compendium of Public Opinion* (New York: Facts On File, 1988), p. 162.
8. "Outlook on Social Issues," *American Enterprise*, 2, no. 5 (September/October 1991).

9. Caplow et al., p. 562.
10. Ladd.
11. Richard Reeves, "Patriotism to Make the Heart Vibrate," *New York Times*, July 4, 1981.
12. John Schaar, "What Is Patriotism?" *Nation*, 252, no. 3 (July 15/22, 1991), pp. 75–76.
13. Wecter, p. 489.
14. Ibid.
15. Quoted in Curti, p. 233.
16. Wecter, p. 490.

EPILOGUE

1. Richard Rorty, "The Unpatriotic Academy." *New York Times*, February 13, 1994, p. 15.
2. *See* Edmund Leites, "Who's an American? Ask Lincoln," *New York Times*, February 12, 1994, p. 15.
3. Quoted in Kammen, p. 648.

For Further Reading

Appel, David H., ed. *An Album for Americans*. New York: Triangle, 1983.

Bodnar, John. *Remaking America: Public Memory, Commemoration and Patriotism in the Twentieth Century*. Princeton, N.J.: Princeton University Press, 1992.

Curti, Merle. *Roots of American Loyalty*. New York: Russell and Russell, 1967.

Grodzins, Morton. *The Loyal and the Disloyal*. New York: World, 1966.

Horwitz, Elinor Lander. *The Bird, the Banner and Uncle Sam*. New York: Lippincott, 1976.

Kammen, Michael. *The Mystic Chords of Memory: The Transformation of Tradition in American Culture*. New York: Knopf, 1991.

Kruthe, Maymie. *What So Proudly We Hail: All about Our American Flag, Monuments and Symbols*. New York: Harper and Row, 1968.

Nye, Russell. *This Almost Chosen People*. Lansing: Michigan State University Press, 1966.

Quaif, Milo, Melvin J. Weig, and Roy E. Appleman. *The History of the United States Flag*. New York: Harper and Row, 1961.

Schlesinger, Arthur Jr. *The Disuniting of America: Reflections on a Multicultural Society*. New York: Norton, 1992.

Wecter, Dixon. *The Hero in America*. New York: Scribners, 1972.

White, Theodore. *America in Search of Itself*. New York: Harper and Row, 1982.

INDEX

About the Author

Gerald Leinwand, a frequent lecturer and consultant to school systems, was formerly president of Western Oregon State College. He is the author of many books on history and social issues, including *Heroism in America*; *American Immigration: Should the Open Door Be Closed?*; and *Do We Need a New Constitution?* for Franklin Watts.

Dr. Leinwand lives in New York City.